School Improvement in Practice

To Paul, Sarah, Peter, Ben, Chloe, Charlie, Jack, Tom, Ben, Dan, Jody and their children's children.

School Improvement
in Practice:
Schools Make A Difference Project

Edited by

Kate Myers

Falmer Press

(A member of the Taylor & Francis Group)
London • Washington, D.C.

UK   The Falmer Press, 4 John Street, London WC1N 2ET
USA   The Falmer Press, Taylor & Francis Inc., 1900 Frost Road, Suite 101, Bristol, PA 19007

First published in 1996

A catalogue record for this book is available from the British Library

Library of Congress Cataloging-in-Publication Data are available on request

ISBN 0 7507 0439 x cased
ISBN 0 7507 0440 3 paper

Jacket design by Caroline Archer

Typeset in 11/13 pt Garamond by
Graphicraft Typesetters Ltd., Hong Kong.

Printed in Great Britain by Burgess Science Press, Basingstoke on paper which has a specified pH value on final paper manufacture of not less than 7.5 and is therefore 'acid free'.

Contents

Acknowledgements

Acknowledgements are due to the education department of the London borough of Hammersmith and Fulham for having the foresight and courage to mount an innovative and exciting project in a climate where such initiatives have not been easy to introduce or sustain.

The contributions of the heads, staff and students of all the project schools was the essential ingredient to its success as was the continual support from colleagues at the Institute of Education, London University, especially Louise Stoll, and the generosity of colleagues in other schools and education establishments. It was the hard work, good humour and perseverance of the project coordinators, the assistance and cooperation of many colleagues in the education department, especially Yvonne Mullarkey the SMAD administrator, the ongoing reassurance from the project evaluator and, in particular, the support, experience and wisdom of Joan Farrelly, that kept me going through usually enjoyable and often challenging times! Much appreciation is due to the following for constructive comments on early drafts: James Learmonth, Agnes McMahon, Harvey Goldstein, Louise Stoll, Anna Clarkson and to Sue Adler for compiling a user-friendly index. Finally, the late Desmond Nuttall was involved in early discussions about SMAD and his conviction that schools could make a difference and his advice about how to demonstrate this, informed the way the project operated.

Foreword

'It is better to light a candle than curse the darkness.'
(Chinese Proverb)

When the Inner London Education Authority (ILEA) was disbanded in 1990, thirteen separate education authorities were created in its place. Two years after its creation, in partnership with all of its secondary schools, one of these fledgling LEAs instigated a school improvement project, called *Schools Make a Difference* (SMAD). The story of SMAD is the focus of this book.

Introduction

The Local Context

When the Inner London Education Authority (ILEA) was disbanded in 1990, thirteen separate education authorities, including Hammersmith and Fulham, were created in its place. Hammersmith and Fulham shares many of the characteristics typically associated with inner-cities. Many of the traditional manufacturing activities of this part of London have left, with a consequent loss of manual jobs. Unemployment is high. Much of the housing stock was built in the nineteenth century and still needs extensive repair. Large, older, council estates suffer from poor environments which exacerbate the social and economic problems of those who live there. Owner occupation has greatly expanded in the last twenty years and has been accompanied by considerable socio-economic change. However, the issue of the provision of 'affordable' housing has become very important within areas of multiple deprivation in the borough.

Overall, the borough has the fourth highest population density of any London borough. A fifth of the borough's population comes from the ethnic minority communities. The largest ethnic minority group is the Irish followed by people from the Black Caribbean, Black African, Pakistani, Bangladeshi, Indian and other Asian communities. More than eighty languages are used in the borough. In May 1994, 44 per cent of secondary school students were eligible for free school meals — a rise of 6 per cent compared with January 1993, when the *Schools Make A Difference* (SMAD) project started. This compares with a national figure of 17.6 per cent of secondary pupils eligible for free school meals. Labour has a substantial majority of seats on the local council.

The Schools

The schools involved in SMAD were:

Burlington Danes School
Fulham Cross Secondary School

The Hammersmith School (since renamed The Phoenix High
   School)
Henry Compton Secondary School
Hurlingham and Chelsea Secondary School
Lady Margaret School
Sacred Heart High School
St Mark's Church of England School

There are eight LEA secondary schools in the borough (plus one grant-maintained school). Four of the LEA schools are single sex, three girls' and one boys'. Four of the eight schools are voluntary aided, three Church of England and one Roman Catholic. One of the schools has a sixth form and the others have a common sixth form arrangement off-site. When the project was first discussed with the heads, two of them were in their second year of headship. During SMAD three heads left the local authority, two schools had acting heads and two newly appointed heads started their new jobs during the last term of the project.

The Director of Education revealed in her recent annual report that soon after her appointment in 1989 she was informed that overall the level of education in the secondary sector was not satisfactory.

> . . . in broad terms, based on unpublished information given to the Director and Chief Inspector by the local ILEA inspectors before abolition by the Regional HMI, and by the initial monitoring work done by our own Inspectorate in our secondary schools, it would be reasonable to say that only 2 of the schools at the time of transfer were not cause of some concern and a further 3 were a cause for considerable concern. It can therefore be seen that the size of the task in relation to the secondary sector was considerable.[1] (The Director of Education's Annual Report 1993/4 Part D. p3, 2.3).

Given this context, the newly appointed Chief Inspector wanted to initiate a school improvement project immediately but the budgetary situation dictated that this idea had to be held in abeyance. In the meantime a new inspection and advisory service was set up that con-

---

[1] Acknowledging that examination results are only one measure (*albeit* an important one) of a school's success, the new local authority was nevertheless concerned about this indicator. ILEA used an overall performance score (7 points for a grade A to 1 point for a grade G) which revealed a borough average of 18.7 in 1988. The scores ranged from 13.4 in the lowest achieving school to 22 in the highest. These scores compared with an ILEA average of 17.7.

sisted of twenty-three (since reduced to fourteen) inspectors. This service confirmed concerns about the standards in some of the secondary schools. In 1992 the education department was invited by the council to bid for funds to support innovative projects. The Chief Inspector and Director immediately resurrected their idea of a two-year school improvement project, which was endorsed by all the secondary heads, and by the local political members. SMAD consequently came into existence in January 1993. The Chief Inspector's perspective of this story is described in Chapter 2.

During the two-year project, four of the eight schools underwent Ofsted Inspections. For most of the project it was anticipated that St Mark's school would move to a neighbouring borough, but following a critical Ofsted report the Secretary of State refused permission for this to happen and during the last part of SMAD, because of surplus numbers of pupils within the local authority, the school was threatened with closure. The Hammersmith School was deemed as requiring special measures following its Ofsted inspection in February 1994, and Hurlingham and Chelsea, although described as a failing school in the pilot Ofsted inspections during the first year of SMAD, 'passed' the subsequent inspection the following year.

These were times of change and turbulence in education and on occasions it seemed to be particularly turbulent in the London borough of Hammersmith and Fulham. Attempting to instigate a school improvement project in this context could be described as foolhardy. An alternative description, and one most of us involved in SMAD believed, is that it is only by taking hold of the initiative ourselves that we can have any impact. It is easy in this climate to be forever reacting and just coping with other people's agendas. Hammersmith and Fulham took the brave step of mounting a well-resourced initiative aimed at empowering schools to look outside the immediate and, based on their own individual needs, plan and implement strategies to lay the foundations for raising student levels of attainment, achievement and morale.

About the Book

SMAD was based on research from four fields — school effectiveness, school improvement, managing change and action research.

The findings of this research are discussed in the 'Prologue'. In Chapter 1, Christine Whatford, the Director of Education in the borough, explains why she believes that in spite of some views to the contrary, LEAs continue to have an important role to play in this climate, and what that role is. In her view this role is strategic, resourcing, support and monitoring and she illustrates how, through the SMAD project, Hammersmith and Fulham exercised this role in these four areas. On the whole she feels that the project was of great benefit to the schools, but like some of the other contributors, she questions whether schools experiencing severe difficulties can make the best use of this kind of support.

In the following chapter, Joan Farrelly, the deputy director/chief inspector at the time SMAD was created, describes how the idea of a school improvement project became a reality. She describes the disparate nature of the schools when Hammersmith and Fulham took over from the Inner London Education Authority (ILEA) in 1990 and how when the opportunity became available to fund an innovative project it was seized with alacrity. She reflects candidly on the successes and shortcomings of the project and concludes her chapter by addressing the question of whether she would do the same thing in the same way again, and what she has learned from the experience.

My chapter (Chapter 3) relates what happened during the project from the project manager's perspective. I describe setting up the structure of SMAD and the strategies employed centrally and in the schools, including those directly affecting staff, students, parents and improving the learning environment. At the end of the chapter I consider some of the issues arising from such a project such as the tensions that arise for an external facilitator trying to maintain the appropriate balance of pressure and support; attempting to work on long-term development issues in a context of constant changes in key personnel; external pressures and agendas (particularly Ofsted); and the 'state of readiness' to address issues of improvement of the different schools.

The two following chapters are accounts from participating schools, Burlington Danes and St Mark's. In Chapter 4, David Lees the deputy head at Burlington Danes, discusses his initial, less than enthusiastic reactions when he first heard about the 'yet another acronymed initiative' and what happened that made him change his mind. Sue Gregory, the coordinator at the school, describes what Burlington Danes attempted to do and what it succeeded in doing as part of the SMAD initiative and addresses some of the issues facing an internal change agent who is also a teacher with a full timetable and other responsibilities. In Chapter 5, Lesley Mortimer, the head of St Mark's school, explains how the project coincided with a period of uncertainty and high drama at the school concluding with the recent decision to close it. She is nevertheless very positive about the SMAD experience and describes some of the inset and visits undertaken as well as the impact the project had on the school. She suggests that although the school will be no more, SMAD will have imprinted itself on the collective memory of staff and students alike. Donna Drake, one of the coordinators at St Mark's, chronicles in detail how the project started at the school and what, in her view, it accomplished.

In Chapter 6, Keith Pocklington, the SMAD evaluator, discusses the project from the external perspective. He reviews its main achievements, including the benefits for teachers and pupils, and discusses the factors aiding and hindering the development of the project. The central section of his chapter focuses on the main developments that occurred in the schools. He identifies three areas in which intended developments were slow to come about and raises a series of key questions and issues for consideration by all who are interested in school improvement.

The final contribution from Patrick Leeson, the acting chief inspector, describes the initiative from an inspector's perspective and explains how the local authority is supporting the schools following the formal ending of the project.

All the chapters are intended to be freestanding but it is hoped that, read in its entirety, *School Improvement in Practice: Schools Make A Difference*, presents an honest and frank account of one borough's attempt to work with its schools to improve the quality of the school experience and student outcomes.

Kate Myers
May 1995

Reference

Education Department Annual Report (1993/4) Parts — *A The Chief Inspector's Report; B Review of 1993/4 Annual Development Plans; C Revision to the 1994/5 Annual Development Plan; & D The Director of Education's Annual Report*, Education Department, Hammersmith and Fulham.

Prologue *Research in Practice*

Kate Myers

Introduction

The *Schools Make a Difference* (SMAD) project was underpined by education research from four different areas: school effectiveness, school improvement, managing change and action research. (As well as using this research it was hoped that the experience of trying to apply it in practice would add to our knowledge base and be of use to colleagues making similar attempts in the future.) This chapter summarizes the research upon which SMAD was based.

Practitioners often have ambivalent feelings about academic research. These include a belief that 'academics' in their rarefied ivory towers, may have wonderful suggestions but no real idea what it means to engage Year 9 week after week (particularly on a wet Friday afternoon). These academics are sometimes both despised and envied for their apparent lifestyle which gives them the luxury of reading and reflecting (as part of their job!) and then making astute comments about the state of . . . while teachers are faced with the daily drudge of getting on and doing it. Furthermore at times, it seems that some of the so-called 'findings' are only common sense and consequently do not justify the time and money required.

On the other hand, many of us complain when changes are imposed from above without any *evidence* that they are likely to improve the current situation. On these occasions, we know that sane and thorough research is much needed. No doubt some research has been mainly of esoteric interest: some research may have no obvious immediate relevance but may nevertheless be important. However, there is also a considerable amount that is 'teacher-friendly' and has direct relevance to work in schools. Good educational research is accessible (in order to inform our practice) and inspiring (in order for us to want to use it to inform our practice).

School Effectiveness

Research that shows that schools can make a difference to the quality of the educational experience and the educational outcomes of its students, has been available for some time. The schools that make a difference for the better are generally described as *effective schools* and those that do the reverse as *ineffective schools*. This of course begs the question of what 'better' means and how we can recognize it. Most commonly it is taken to mean academic success, though even here we have little hard research evidence about the precise means whereby some schools appear to produce higher achievements than others. Even in the limited number of studies that have been able to take account of the learning context fully, including access to some form of prior achievement, our knowledge tends to be of a general rather than specific nature. Mortimore (1991) defines an effective school 'as one in which pupils progress further than might be expected from consideration of its intake' (p. 9). In other words, an effective school 'adds extra value to its students' outcomes in comparison with other schools serving similar intakes' (Sammons, Hillman and Mortimore, 1995, p. 3). It is important to note that schools are not always as effective with all their students. For example, some schools may do well with low achievers or Afro-Caribbean girls but not so well for other groups within the school (Nuttall *et al*, 1988).

There have now been numerous studies of effective schools in many countries around the world. Characteristics of effective schools in poor countries are similar to those in richer ones with one exception: not surprisingly extra resources can have a far greater impact in poorer countries (Lockheed, 1995). However, it is interesting to note that so far although much attention has been paid to ineffective schools, particularly those in this country deemed by the Office for Standards in Education (OFSTED or, as now commonly known, Ofsted) as 'requiring special measures', they have not in themselves been the focus of much research (Reynolds, 1994).

Pam Sammons and her colleagues (1995) have recently undertaken a review of school effectiveness research for Ofsted. According to this paper, researchers believe that schools can make a significant difference (depending on the researcher, between 8–18 per cent) to student outcomes even when background factors such as age, sex and social class are taken into account. Translated into practice this can mean the difference between schools' value-added scores of between seven grade 'E' results or seven grade 'C' results at GCSE (Thomas and Mortimore, 1994). Preceded by a severe health warning, that alerts readers to the dangers of 'quick fixes' and the importance of context (for example, primary/secondary, national differences, nature of intake), Sammons *et al.* have identified eleven common features that appear to be connected with the process and characteristics of more effective schools:

1. Professional leadership
2. Shared vision and goals
3. A learning environment
4. Concentration on teaching and learning
5. Purposeful teaching
6. High expectations
7. Positive reinforcement
8. Monitoring progress
9. Pupil rights and responsibilities
10. Home–school partnership
11. A learning organization

(It is worth remembering that although the research studies reviewed by Pam Sammons and her colleagues indicated that these characteristics exist in the more effective schools, the presence of them *per se*, does not of course guarantee that a school is effective. More information is needed about how these characteristics interact before this judgment can be made.)

1 *Professional Leadership*

Almost all studies with the exception of those that have taken place in the Netherlands, where the headteacher's role is somewhat different, have drawn attention to the importance of the head's leadership role. Three characteristics are associated with successful leaders:

- they are firm and purposeful
- they adopt a participative approach
- they are the leading professional.

Effective leaders successfully find the balance between autocratic and democratic styles of management. They have a vision but know when it is proper to involve others in the decision-making process. They are also concerned and knowledgable about teaching and learning and are highly visible around the school.

2   *Shared Vision and Goals*

Shared vision and goals involves a unity of purpose, consistency of practice and collegiality and collaboration.

> Both school effectiveness research and evaluations of school improvement programmes show that consensus on the values and goals of the school is associated with improved educational outcomes. (Sammons *et al.*, 1995, p. 11)

Teachers in effective schools participate in making the rules and then carry them out consistently. A school where collegiality and collaboration are apparent amongst the staff is not one where they necessarily go to the pub together, but it is one where teachers have professional respect for each other and work well together for a common purpose that is to improve the teaching programme.

3   *A Learning Environment*

A learning environment is one with an orderly atmosphere and an attractive working environment. The school is calm, students can get on with their work and the building is an attractive place in which to work.

4   *Concentration on Teaching and Learning*

Effective schools maximize learning time by spending time wisely. There is a positive correlation between student outcomes and the proportion of the day spent on academic subjects and, just as important, the proportion of time spent in lessons devoted to learning (time on task) and interaction with pupils. In addition there is an academic emphasis in such schools and a focus on achievement.

5   *Purposeful Teaching*

'The quality of teaching is at the heart of successful schooling' (Sammons *et al.*, 1985, p. 15). In successful schools, teachers are well organized and lessons are planned in advance, are well structured and have clear objectives which are communicated to the pupils. Successful teachers are sensitive to differences in the learning styles of the pupils and adapt their teaching style accordingly.

6 High Expectations

Studies show a strong relationship between high expectations and effective learning. Low expectations are often an important factor in underachievement particularly for students in disadvantaged urban schools. Where teachers communicate their high expectations to pupils, there is a consequent effect on pupils' self-esteem. When expectations are high, pupils are more likely to be provided with intellectually challenging lessons.

7 Positive Reinforcement

Although good discipline is a prerequisite in a successful school, this is not obtained by too frequent use of punishment. Appropriate positive rewards and feedback are much more effective.

8 Monitoring Progress

Monitoring pupil performance and evaluating school performance are both essential aspects of monitoring progress. In successful schools, monitoring pupils' progress is appropriate (for example, record keeping of strengths and weaknesses) and not too frequent. Headteachers are involved in evaluating the school's performance and information gleaned from these evaluations is used actively and informs planning.

9 Pupils' Rights and Responsibilities

Many studies have linked pupils' self-esteem with their achievement. Pupils in effective schools feel they are respected and that their needs are understood and met with appropriate responses. In these schools, pupils are given responsibility and have some control over what happens to them in school.

10 Home–school Partnership

Studies generally show that cooperation between home and school has positive effects. However, the effects of parental involvement in school life are not quite as clear cut although several studies in the primary phase show a positive link between achievement in reading and parental involvement.

11   A Learning Organization

In an effective school, everyone—pupils and adults—is a learner, and learning takes place at all levels in the organization. Effective inset is school based, classroom focused and ongoing.

Sammons and her colleagues make the point that this research base helps us identify the characteristics of effective schools but does not help us apply that knowledge. For help in this area we need to turn to the literature of school improvement and managing change.

School Improvement

According to Hillman and Stoll (1994):

> The ultimate aim of school improvement is to achieve a range of goals that will enhance learning, achievement and development amongst pupils. (p. 2)

As with the school effectiveness research field, there have now been numerous studies in a range of countries aimed at helping schools 'get better'. For example, in 1989 over half of all American school districts ran improvement programmes based upon, or linked to, the effective schools knowledge base. (Reynolds, Hopkins and Stoll, 1993). They were attempting to utilize the research on school effectiveness to improve their schools.

The OECD-sponsored (Organization for Economic Cooperation and Development) International School Improvement project defines school improvement as

> a systematic, sustained effort aimed at change in learning conditions and other related internal conditions in one or more schools, with the ultimate aim of accomplishing educational goals more effectively. (van Velzen, 1985)

The main point here is that the change is not any old change. It is *systematic* and *sustained.* Increasingly commentators emphasize the importance of change being directly related to student learning.

> We define school improvement as an approach to educational change that has the twin purposes of enhancing pupil achievement and strengthening the school's capacity for managing change . . . school improvement approaches to educational change seek to enhance pupil outcomes. (Hopkins, Stoll, Myers, Learmonth and Durman, 1995)

Recent school improvement initiatives have concentrated on raising achievement, (for example the RAISE project, 'Raising Achievement In Shropshire Education'). With open enrolment and the publication of examination league tables there is an increasing danger of defining achievement solely as improved examination results. Unquestionably, examination results are important. For many students they are the passport to a different lifestyle. However, they are not the only purpose of school (Myers, 1994a). David Hargreaves and his colleagues proposed that schools should be concerned with four kinds of achievement in their 1984 'Improving Secondary Schools' report to the Inner London Education Authority:

Aspect 1   Dealing with the capacity to remember and use facts;
Aspect 2   Practical and spoken skills;
Aspect 3   Personal and social skills;
Aspect 4   Motivation and self-confidence.

School improvement initiatives concerned with long-term benefits should address all these aspects — not just the first one. It is important to remember that a student could achieve excellent examination results — even using a value-added measure — but could have an appalling experience of schooling, affecting their self-esteem and confidence. For example, unfortunately it is not uncommon for students to be subjected to racial and/or sexual harassment (Mahony, 1985; Kelly, 1991; Stein, Marshall and Tropp, 1993; AAUW, 1993). It is vital therefore that school improvement considers the *quality* of the school experience as well as quantifiable outcomes and, of course, how to evaluate this experience.

School improvement does not have to be based on the deficit model of schools. Hopkins and Ainscow neatly sum this up with their motto, 'You don't have to be sick to get better'. In other works, however good we are we could still get better. Reynolds *et al.* (1993) offer the following useful summary of how school improvement initiatives have changed over the last thirty years (see Table 1.1). The characteristics listed in Table 1.1 are of course trends rather than a definitive statements. Nevertheless they do convey different approaches to school improvement. The early work in this field was done *to* schools, assumed

Table 1.1 *Characteristics of two school improvement paradigms*

Orientation	1960s 'top down'	1980s 'bottom up'
Knowledge base	elite knowledge	practitioner knowledge
Target	organization or curriculum based	process based
Outcomes	pupil outcome orientated	school process orientated
Goals	outcomes as given	outcomes as problematic
Focus	school	teacher
Methodology of evaluation	quantitative	qualitative
Site	outside school	within school
Focus	part of school	whole school

an accurate and unproblematic knowledge base and concentrated on quantifiable student outcomes (usually test scores). In the 1980s much school improvement work was qualitative, initiated by practitioners, based on their experiences, concentrated on processes and often focused on the individual teacher rather than the whole school. In the 1990s there appears to be a realistic and logical move to concentrate on whichever of the characteristics listed above are appropriate to the endeavour rather than those that neatly fit a particular paradigm.

Projects around the country (Myers and Stoll, 1993) have demonstrated that there is an increasing awareness at central government, local government and school level that school improvement is pertinent and relevant to current needs — a potential real merging of the distinct 'top down' 'bottom up' approaches. I use the word 'potential' because although there is some agreement about the need for school improvement there is still a considerable difference in the aims and goals of some of the parties concerned. Many of these projects have been run in partnership with institutions of higher education (for example the 'Lewisham School Improvement' project run in conjunction with the London Institute of Education; Staffordshire LEA's 'Two Towns' project with the Education Department at Keele University; Cambridge Institute of Education's 'Improving the Quality of Education for All' (IQEA) project, working with several LEAs and individual schools). These *partnerships* exemplify a different attitude to research where the research base is of prime importance and underpins the philosophy of all these projects. However, it has to be accessible and of practical use to those attempting to make changes in their schools. Consequently academics from these institutions of higher education are making concerted attempts to demystify the research and work in association with colleagues at the chalk-face.

Evaluating the targets and outcomes of these projects is not without problems but increasingly researchers are concentrating on quantifiable student outcomes *as well* as process or 'ethos' indicators (MacBeath, Thomson, Arrowsmith and Forbes, 1992). The process involved is deemed important but not an end in itself. The importance of change at classroom level as well as whole school is recognized. Although recent government policies have encouraged schools to become more competitive with each other, there is also an understanding that school improvement in isolation is almost a contradiction in terms. Schools need each other to share ideas and good practice. They need each other to stimulate enquiry and comparison, to prevent complacency and insularity.

> Essentially any endeavour which also seeks to evaluate its success *must* do so co-operatively and comparatively. To know whether what we are doing is the best way of doing it or whether the results we observe can ever be attributed to our intervention *per se*, we have to compare ourselves with others. This is the essence of social research and it should also inform our practice in the sense that we are continually involved in comparative evaluation. School improvement is not simply about sending in a plumber to mend the leaking toilet but at best is part of a continuing activity trying to understand what works and why it should do so. It is for these reasons that a political climate of 'high-stakes' competition is contrary to good school improvement practice and poses a particular dilemma for those engaged in such work. (Goldstein, 1995)

As well as needing each other, schools need resources to initiate and support change.

> To carry out a change or improvement always involves an increment of *extra* resources . . . Change, by definition, cannot be managed through the status quo level of resources. It makes new demands, creates unsolved problems, is resource hungry. (Louis and Miles, 1992, p. 239).

Resources in this context include equipment, time, personnel and training. Louis and Miles make the point that *how* the money is used (and how decisions are made about this issue) is as important as how much money is available and that existing resources can often be reallocated without adding new ones. Nevertheless, 'no new resources, little change' (ibid, p. 261). The long-term consequences of the current reduction in resources, being experienced by many schools, cannot be overestimated. School improvement then is:

- a recognition that schools can and should get better;
- that pupil outcomes are paramount but this does not just mean examination results;
- that there are a variety of ways of achieving these outcomes;
- that the experiences of other schools cannot be considered as blueprints but can be of use and relevance to those attempting improvement;
- that appropriate resources are essential;
- and that together we can make a difference to the lives of our pupils.

It may be trite but nevertheless it is true that:

All Improvement is Change
But Not All Change is Improvement.
(Stoll, 1992)

The literature on managing change can help us implement planned change that is aimed solely at improvement.

Managing Change

Reformers have the idea that change can be achieved by brute sanity.
(George Bernard Shaw, quoted by Fullan, 1987)

There was a time (within living memory) when schools were faced with occasional centrally dictated change — for example the Raising of the School Leaving Age (ROSLA), the introduction of the Certificate of Secondary Education (CSE), and later the General Certificate of Secondary Education (GCSE). The changes may not have been universally agreed but time was spent on consultation and then implementation. On the whole, schools coped with these sort of innovations sporadically and one at a time. In the last few years, however, schools have been faced with centrally dictated multiple and multifarious changes. Not all of these changes have been popular and not all of them have led to improvement. Nevertheless it seems that in the world as it is now, continuous change is going to be the order of the day. ('Order' is perhaps not the most appropriate of words . . .)

Other institutions are similarly affected:

> Educational managers are not alone in facing major changes.
> The same kinds of pressures are also affecting business, indus-
> try and commerce. (Bennett, Crawford and Riches, 1992, p. 2)

Planning and managing change, whether centrally imposed or internally initiated, at least gives the institution concerned some control over
what is happening. It also allows the institution to mould the change,
as far as possible, to suit its own needs.

In the 1960s and early 1970s, innovations such as some of the early
Schools Council projects tended to rely on the Research, Development
and Dissemination (RD&D) model. It was envisaged that if the change
had been well researched and then developed in pilot schools, once
everyone had heard about it they would all understand and agree with
it and be enthusiastic about implementing it. In fact the result was not
large-scale adoption of proposed changes and even when some of the
changes were taken on by schools they were adapted and adopted to
suit their own needs. Subsequent changes were often not those envisaged by the original developers of the innovation. There appeared to
be no such thing as 'teacher-proof' materials.

RD&D is a technological model that takes little account of the fact
that most human beings are not entirely rational and, even when they
are, one person's rationality is not necessarily the same as another's.
The model may be appropriate for agricultural research but is somewhat flawed when human-beings are the focus. People have different
perspectives and different vested interests. With the failure occurring at
the implementation and dissemination stage of many large-scale projects,
researchers such as House (1981) started to consider political and cultural perspectives alongside the technological ones that influenced the
adoption of change. They stressed the importance of taking account of
local differences and teacher resistance. Innovators realized the importance of *process* as well as *content.*

> Fundamentally optimistic, the perspective assumes that barriers
> to innovation can be anticipated and managed. (Firestone and
> Corbett, 1988, p. 323)

Michael Fullan shares this perspective. He describes the field as 'the
management of change for achieving successful outcomes' (Fullan, 1987).
He makes six observations about change.

1   *Brute sanity* (based on Shaw's quote, above) — 'Brute sanity overpromises, overrationalises and consequently results in unfulfilled dreams and frustrations which discourage people from sustaining their efforts and from taking on future change projects' (Fullan, 1987, p. 16). Fullan suggests that conviction in the certainty of the change can get it on the agenda but it is not an effective strategy for implementing change.

2   *Overload* — it is impossible to implement everything that is supposed to be implemented because:
    there are too many changes;
    implementation is often attempted too early;
    initiatives are often too ambitious;
    and multiple projects are introduced in an uncoordinated way.

3   *Implementing the implementation plan* — the plans themselves can be problematic. Everything we know about the implementation of curriculum innovations must be applied to developing implementation plans.

4   *Content versus process* — both are important and need their own implementation strategies.

5   *Pressure and support* — a combination of both is necessary: 'Support without pressure can waste resources; pressure without support creates alienation' (p. 17).

6   *Change equals learning* — we need to utilize our knowledge about how adults learn when designing and carrying out strategies for implementation.

Fullan suggests that there are three broad phases of change; initiation, implementation and institutionalization.

At the *initiation* stage Fullan suggests four requirements:

i)   the educational need should be linked to an agenda of political (high profile) need;
ii) a clear model should exist for the proposed change;
iii) there must be a strong advocate for the change;
iv) there should be an early active initiation establishing commitment.

At the *implementation* stage, critical needs include:

   i)   the involvement of a group — needed to oversee the implementation plan and carry it through;

  ii)   the correct balance of pressure and support;

 iii)   early rewards for those involved;

  v)   ongoing inset, to maintain commitment as behaviours often change before beliefs.

At the *institutionalization* stage — an innovation will be more successful if:

   i)   it becomes imbedded into the fabric of everyday practice;

  ii)   it is clearly linked to classroom practice;

 iii)   it is used in several classrooms and schools;

 iv)   it is not contending with conflicting priorities;

  v)   new staff are exposed to inset to consolidate commitment.

Fullan concludes his article with the following tips (1987, pp. 15–18):

   i)   Effective entrepreneurs exploit multiple innovations.

  ii)   Overcome the 'if only' problem, for example, 'If only the government would stop introducing so many policies...' (*Authors note — NB This was written in 1987!*).

 iii)   Manage multiple innovations, 'Do two well and the others as well as possible'.

 iv)   Get better at implementation planning — more by doing than planning. Start small but think big.

  v)   Beware of implementation dip, i.e., the risk of temporary de-skilling as innovators learn new skills.

 vi)   Remember that research shows behaviour changes first and changes in belief follow.

 vii)   Recognize that project leaders need to have a vision of content and process and the relationship between the two which will promote change. To have a vision of content change without a vision of process change is an example of 'brute sanity'.

viii)   Acknowledge the importance of ownership and commitment and that ownership is a process where commitment is increasingly acquired.

Fullan's practical, common-sense approach to managing change is reassuring and helpful for those involved in change projects such as

SMAD. However, it is also important to remember that he writes from a North American perspective and we need to interpret his work within the current prevailing cultural context in this country. The final research field that we drew from was that of action research.

Action Research

There are many definitions of action research. Most of them have some reference to the involvement of practitioners and the significance of reflective practice. The term 'action' implies some change to the status quo and the word 'research' 'introduces the notion of systematic enquiry, rather than just reflection on action' (McMahon, 1993, p. 6). John Elliott suggests that it might be defined as, 'the study of a social situation with a view to improving the quality of action within it' (Elliott, 1991, p. 69).

It is widely believed that the term 'action research' originated in the work done in North America in the 1920s and 1930s by John Collier, a Commissioner of Indian Affairs, and Kurt Lewin who was a social psychologist (McMahon, 1993). The importance of social scientists working *with* practitioners was emphasized in the work of both these men.

> Practitioners had to be involved in action research not only to use the tools of social science in addressing their concerns, but also because their participation would make them more aware of the need for the action program chosen and more personally invested in the process of change. (Oja and Smulyan, 1989, p. 3)

The work of Lawrence Stenhouse — who directed the Schools' Council's 'Humanities Curriculum' project and subsequently established the Centre for Applied Research in Education (CARE) at the University of East Anglia — was very influential on the action research movement in education in this country.

> He argued that only when teachers adopted a research stance to their own teaching would high quality and effective curriculum development be achieved. (McMahon, 1993, p. 3)

For Stenhouse and other writers who followed him, teachers' involvement in action research was critical.

> Improved practice results from practitioner participation in the investigation of actions and issues of immediate importance. (Oja and Smulyan, 1989, p. 1)

In a paper written in 1978, John Elliott, who worked with Stenhouse, suggested that action research in schools is concerned with everyday, practical problems experienced by teachers.

> Teacher–research[er] action research does not typically start with hypotheses derived from the research literature, and is not usually concerned to contribute to the corpus of social science knowledge and theory. (Kelly, 1985, p. 131)

In theory (but not always in practice) when teachers are involved in this type of research they are empowered; they are informed partners and in some cases in complete control of the initiative. The notion of the teacher as a researcher is linked to, but not the same as, action research. As John Elliott (1978) points out, action research may be carried out by the teachers themselves *or* by someone they commission to carry it out for them. Emancipatory action research emphasizes the importance of the role of the participants.

> In action research, all those involved in the research process should come to participate equally in all its phases of planning, acting, observing and reflecting. In this, action research is democratic: it recognises that conditions for investigating the truth of knowledge-claims are also the conditions for democratic participation in critical discussion. (Carr and Kemmis, 1986, p. 199)

According to Sharon Nodie Oja and Lisa Smulyan (1989, p. 12), there are four basic elements of action research. They are its:

1 Collaborative nature
2 Focus on practical problems
3 Emphasis on professional development
4 Need for a project structure which provides participants with time and support for open communication.

In addition, Cohen and Manion (1989) suggest that it is self-evaluative, the effects of strategies used are constantly monitored, and the strategies are consequently modified. Elliott emphasizes the importance of action research leading to improvements in practice (McMahon, 1993).

Stemming from Kurt Lewin's model, action research is often described as being a cyclical process with four key steps (McMahon, 1993):

- Planning
- Action
- Reconnaissance
- Re-planning (re-starting the cycle)

According to Carr and Kemmis:

> Some of what passes for action research today fails to meet the requirements . . . for action research: it is not concerned with the systematic investigation of a social or educational practice, it is not participatory or collaborative, and it does not employ the spiral of self-reflection. (1986, p. 201)

Was SMAD Action Research?

A key point about action research is that the researchers are themselves involved in the action. (McMahon, 1995)

In the SMAD project there was an external evaluator but other participants were responsible for originating, negotiating and implementing interventions and then researching their impact. These 'others' included myself as project manager and the coordinators. From the beginning we were all aware of this dual role and established methods of recording and data collection. Being aware of the need to do something, however, is no guarantee that it will happen. One of the early casualties was the diaries that we had all agreed to keep. I managed to sustain intermittent entries throughout the project, but though several coordinators started enthusiastically producing detailed and pertinent commentaries on what was happening, none of them perservered with method of data collection. (A similar problem occured with this method of recording on my previous project and it is perhaps unrealistic to expect hard-pressed teachers, bombarded with numerous pressures, to do additional writings.) We did, however, all keep minutes of all meetings records of visits, produce interim reports and photograph almost anything that moved (and much that did not). In addition four of the coordinators submitted accounts of their work for accreditation towards a higher diploma.

The overall research problem was given, that is raising student levels of attainment, achievement and morale, but within that broad framework the strategies and processes used were decided by the individual schools. During the project, the coordinators organized the school-based identification of issues and, through the project proformas (see Chapter 3 for more details of this proforma), planned their intervention and their anticipated success criteria. Action research is usually thought of as being cyclical and throughout the project the impact of these interventions were constantly monitored, reviewed and revised accordingly. (See the coordinators perspective in Chapters 4 and 5.)

According to McMahon:

> Just as there is no single, widely accepted definition of what constitutes action research, so there is no single definition of what constitutes the teacher as researcher. The most general description that one could give is that the teacher researchers are conducting an investigation into some aspect of education which relates to their own work and behaviour while at the same time continuing to work as practitioners in school. (1993, p. 27)

On these terms, the SMAD coordinators were 'teacher researchers' and I hope that the following chapters demonstrate that SMAD fulfills the definitions of action research discussed above and can thus be properly described as an action research project.

Projects

I indicated at the beginning of this chapter that it is hoped that the outcomes from SMAD will be of interest and use to others involved in school improvement and may add to our knowledge base of this important subject. It was, however, never intended that the findings of SMAD would be replicable in other contexts. This book is a case study of one project written by some of the key players. Case studies are presented to illuminate rather than replicate findings. As David Hamilton said:

> It is possible to state that two studies produced identical results. It is never possible to say they were conducted under identical conditions: if they were conducted at the same time, they must have occupied different places; if they were conducted at the

same place they must have occurred at different times. (1980, p. 87)

He goes on to quote Cronbach as suggesting that 'the primary aim of social science should become "interpretation in context" not "generalisation"' (Hamilton, 1980, p. 87).

Both these points are pertinent to the issue of replicability. Firstly, different conditions affect results (and the human variable alone makes each institution different) and secondly, the point of this kind of research is not to make generalizations but to facilitate a deeper understanding of context. Qualitative research using a case-study approach, concentrates on *process* as well as outcomes. This is potentially of considerable practical use to teachers working in different contexts who need to adapt and adopt suggested interventions to suit their own needs.

Action research projects may or may not be established with a view to replicability. Some action research projects involve one teacher perhaps focusing on one aspect of her work who has no intentions that the outcomes of the project will be of any use to anyone but herself. Other projects are much larger scale and may have aspirations to do with replicability. The issue of replicability is affected amongst other things by: the type of project; level of resourcing available; the aims and aspirations; duration; type of school involved; geographical location and local culture; and the 'project effect' (Myers, 1994b).

Types of Project

It is important to distinguish between different types of action projects when addressing the issue of replicability. For example, a single-focus project targeting a homogenous and cohesive group of teachers with readily available network and support facilities — such as an active subject association — may be more easily replicated than a whole school initiative involving a disparate group of stakeholders including staff, students and parents (e.g., SMAD).

Levels of Resourcing

Resourcing projects is a continual source of concern. Extra resources (human and physical) are often the 'carrot' that helps foster interest, encourages schools and make it feasible for them to participate in the first place. The SMAD project was relatively generously funded and it is unlikely that other initiatives will be so well resourced. This could encourage some people to dismiss any findings from SMAD or at least assume they are only possible to achieve in such a well-resourced context. On the other hand, it may be possible to demonstrate that some of the processes and strategies used in the project are feasible in other contexts.

Aims and Aspiration

A project with relatively modest aspirations may be easier to replicate. Although for most projects, 'teacher development is often an aim' some projects are more ambitious. They 'may be judged to have challenged teachers to revise completely the role of a teacher in a classroom. Among educationalists the Humanities Curriculum Project would spring to mind' (Steadman, Parsons and Salter, 1980). As Steadman *et al.* point out, ambitious projects that involve attitudinal as well as behaviour change are more complex to initiate, disseminate and replicate. I think it would be fair to describe SMAD as ambitious and complex.

Duration

The optimum duration of a project tends to depend to some extent on the complexity of its aims — too short a period will not allow sufficient time for induction to the aims, commitment of participants and an emphasis on process; too long a time may result in participant burn-out or loss of enthusiasm. A project that has been allocated an appropriate time span — whatever that is — is likely to be more easily replicated as participants will be willing and able to share in the dissemination process. The formal part of the SMAD project took place during a very short time span. The advantage of this was that minds had to be concentrated and action taken. The disadvantage was that there has not yet been enough time to evaluate the long-term effects of the initiative.

Internal Organization, Structure and Student Intake

Variables such as whether a school is voluntary aided, single-sex, and how it is organized need to be taken into account when considering replicability as does contextual information about the student body (e.g., number of free school meals, parental occupation, ethnicity, ratio of boys/girls, student baseline scores and outcomes). Effective strategies in one type of school will not necessarily be so in another.

Geographical Location and Local Culture

Even a small country such as the UK has immense regional variations (and needs). Local culture also makes a pertinent contribution to the way of life in an area. Education projects concern people and if successful must have some interface with local conditions. It would consequently be ill-advised to attempt to replicate in an inner-city area, a project that had been successful in a rural secondary school without any understanding that some adaptations may be necessary. An even more extreme example (though unfortunately not unknown) is when attempts have been made to transpose initiatives from one country to another — often from the 'developed world' to the 'developing world' with little cognizance of local culture or customs. In these circumstances replicability must be artificial and may be of little use to the participants.

The 'Project Effect'

Participants in successful projects are often said to be affected by the 'project effect'. Although working under tremendous pressure, they have felt special, valued and rewarded. They are key players in an exciting, new and prestigious initiative. Their views at the very least inform the development — they may even be in the vanguard of new research. Although they may at times face frustration when working on aspects of the project (particularly in their role as change agents working with colleagues who are not quite so enthusiastic), in general they feel energized and renewed and have a particular commitment to the initiative. Their personal investment helps make the project work. The real test of an initiative is whether it will survive when the original enthusiasts are no longer involved or whether it was too dependant on charismatic individuals and the 'project effect'. Structures have been established for this to happen following the formal ending of SMAD but of course it remains to be seen how successful they will be.

For all these reasons 'replicability' of projects such as SMAD is not desirable. It may be more appropriate to talk in terms of *transferability* of some of the processes, ideas and strategies involved. These are described in detail in the following chapters.

References

The American Association of University Women (*AAUW*) (1993) *Hostile Hallways: The AAUW Survey on Sexual Harassment in America's Schools*, Washington DC, USA AAUW.

BENNETT, N., CRAWFORD, M., and RICHES, C. (eds) (1992) *Managing Change in Education: Individual and Organizational Perspectives*, Milton Keynes, The Open University Press.

CARR, W. and KEMMIS, S. (1986) *Becoming Critical*, London, Falmer Press.

COHEN, L. and MANION, L. (1989) *Research Methods in Education* (3rd Edn), London, Routledge.

ELLIOTT, J. (1991) *Action Research for Educational Change*, Milton Keynes, Open University Press.

ELLIOTT, J. (1978) 'What is action research in schools?', *Journal of Curriculum Studies*, 10, 4, pp. 355–7.

FIRESTONE, W.A. and CORBETT, H.D. (1988) 'Planned organizational change' in BOYAN, N.J. (ed.) *Handbook of Research on Educational Administration*, New York, Longman.

FULLAN, M. (1987) 'Managing Curriculum Change', in *Curriculum at the Crossroads*, Report of the SCDC Conference on Aspects of Curriculum Change held at Leeds University.

GOLDSTEIN, H. (1995) Private communication.

HAMILTON, D. (1980) 'Some contrasting assumptions about case study research and survey analysis', in SIMONS, H. *Towards a Science of the Singular*, University of East Anglia CARE Occasional Publication No. 10.

HARGREAVES, D. *et al.* (1984) 'Improving secondary schools', Report to the ILEA Committee.

HILLMAN, I. and STOLL, L. (1994) 'Understanding school improvement', in *School Improvement News (SIN) Research Matters No 1*, Institute of Education, University of London.

HOPKINS, D., STOLL, L., MYERS, K., LEARMONTH, J. and DURMAN, H. (1995) *Schools Make A Difference: Practical Strategies for School Improvement*, (Study guide to accompany the Channel 4 series), Southampton, Resource Base Television Centre.

HOUSE, E.R. (1981) 'Three perspectives on educational innovation: technological, political and cultural', in LEHMING, R. and KANE, M. (eds) *Improving Schools: Using What We Know*, Beverley Hills, CA, Sage.

KELLY, A. (1985) 'Action research: What it is and what it can do?', in BURGESS, R. (ed.) *Issues in Education Research: Qualitative Methods*, London, Falmer Press.

KELLY, E. (1991) 'Entitlement for all, race, gender, and ERA: bullying and racial and sexual harassment in schools, *Multicultural Teaching, 10.1*, Trentham Books.

LOCKHEED, M. (1995) 'Effective schools in developing countries: a short and incomplete review.' Keynote address presented at the ICSEI 1995 Congress, Leeuwarden, the Netherlands, January 2–6, 1995.

Louis, K. and Miles, M. (1992) *Improving The Urban High School: What Works And Why*, London, Cassell.

MacBeath, J., Thomson, B., Arrowsmith, J. and Forbes, D. (1992) 'Using ethos indicators in secondary school self-evaluation', *Taking Account of the Views of Pupils, Parents, and Teachers*, HM Inspectors of Schools, The Scottish Office Education Department.

Mahoney, P. (1985) *Schools for the Boys*, London, Hutchinson.

McMahon, A. (1993) *Action Research for School Managers* (Books 1 & 2) NDCEMP, University of Bristol.

McMahon, A. (1995) Private communication.

Mortimore, P. (1991) 'The Nature and Findings of Research on School Effectiveness in the Primary Sector', in (eds) Riddell, S. and Brown, S., *School Effectiveness Research: Its Messages for School Improvement*, The Scottish Office, HMSO.

Myers, K. (1994a) 'Plain truths about higher fliers', *TES*, 4 November.

Myers, K. (1994b) Replicability and sustainibility of small scale initiatives Assignment for Doctor of Education degree, University of Bristol.

Myers, K. and Stoll, L. (1993) 'Mapping the movement', *Education*, 16 July.

Nuttall, D.L., Goldstein, H., Presser, R. and Rasbash, H. (1988) 'Differential school effectiveness', *International Journal of Educational* Research, 13, 7, pp. 769–76.

Oja, S.N. and Smulyan, L. (1989) *Collaborative Action Research: A Developmental Approach*, London, Falmer Press.

Reynolds, D. (1994) 'Inaugural lecture given by Professor David Reynolds on Wednesday, 19 October 1994 at the University of Newcastle Upon Tyne'.

Reynolds, D., Hopkins, D. and Stoll, L. (1993) 'Linking school effectiveness, knowledge and school improvement practice: towards a synergy', *School Effectiveness and School Improvement: An International Journal of Research, Policy and Practice*, Vol. 4, No. 1.

Sammons, P., Hillman, J. and Mortimore, P. (1995) *Key Characteristics of Effective Schools: A Review of School Effectiveness Research* for the Office for Standards in Education by the International School Effectiveness & Improvement Centre, Institute of Education, University of London.

Steadman, S.D., Parsons, C. and Salter B.G. (1980) *Impact and Take-Up Project*, A Second Interim Report to the Schools Council London, Schools Council.

Stein, N., Marshall, N. and Tropp, L. (1993) *Secrets in Public: Sexual Harassment in Our Schools*, Wellesley Center for Research on Women, Wellesley College, USA.

Stoll, L. (1992) 'Making schools matter: linking school effectiveness and school improvement in a Canadian school district' PhD Thesis, Institute of Education, University of London.

Thomas S. and Mortimore P. (1994) 'Report on value added analysis of 1993 GCSE examination results in Lancashire' *Research Papers in Education*.

van Velzen, W. (1985) *Making School Improvement Work: A Conceptual Guide to Practice*, Leuven, Belgium, Acco Publishers.

1 The Director's View

Christine Whatford

The Role of the LEA in Improvement

The last five years has been a time of tremendous change and development in education and part of that change has been in the role that the local education authority (LEA) plays in the education system. Broadly speaking, with the introduction of local management of schools (LMS), as decision making moves closer to the point of service delivery, the role of the local education authority has become less 'hands on' and more strategic. This change was summed up in the title of the Audit Commissions study in 1989 'Losing an Empire, Finding a Role: The LEA of the Future.' The six areas the that Audit Commission prophetically forecast would form the basis of the LEA role were:

1) A leader, articulating a vision of what the education service is trying to achieve.
2) A partner, supporting schools and helping them to fulfil this vision.
3) A planner, of facilities for the future.
4) A provider of information, to the education market, helping people to make informed choices.
5) A regulator, of quality in schools and other institutions.
6) A banker, channelling the funds which enable local institutions to deliver.

Five years later, broadly speaking, those areas have become the core of the LEA's role — although they do not spell out the room for LEAs to act differently and pro-actively according to their local circumstances and to 'add value' to the education delivered to their local communities, both in the school and the non-school sectors.

As far as the London borough of Hammersmith and Fulham is concerned there was never an empire to lose. All the new inner London education authorities were created after the Education Reform Act of 1988: they were established in April 1990. They had no experience of being 'old style' LEAs. The were set up right from the start to operate within a framework of local management of schools. One shouldn't, however, make the mistake of thinking that this meant there was only a minimalist or 'residual' role for the LEA. All the new LEAs by law had to produce an Education Development Plan to submit to the Secretary of State in which they 'set out their stall' as to how they intended to fulfil their responsibilities as LEAs in taking over education in their area. Hammersmith and Fulham saw this as a tremendous opportunity to consult on what its proper role should be in the new, post-ERA (post the Education Reform Act of 1988) world. Through discussions with governors, heads, staff, parents and the local community, that role was defined and refined. It can be summarized as:

1 *Strategic* — Setting the strategic framework for delivering education to the local community in Hammersmith and Fulham, including strategic planning and leadership.

2 *Resourcing* — Making the overall resourcing decisions on how much money will be spent on education locally, including directly providing those parts of the service that are non-statutory and/or outside the LM scheme.

3 *Support* — Providing support to schools to enable them to deliver high quality education to learners.

4 *Monitoring* — Monitoring the quality of education being delivered in schools in partnership with governing bodies.

Given that role, which was negotiated with all the stakeholders in Hammersmith and Fulham, it will come as no surprise that the role of the LEA in bringing about school improvement in Hammersmith and Fulham has been a key one and has operated at all those four levels.

The *Schools Make a Difference* (SMAD) project is one example of the way the LEA exercised that role in those four areas. Other examples were the realization, based on the American research, long before it became commonly accepted as it is now, that Early Years education was key to later achievement and indeed had effects beyond just the education performance. This resulted in a rolling programme of opening new nursery classes funded by the LEA. There was also additional staffing made available to primary schools to support literacy and the introduction of the National Curriculum. These changes took place within the context of the LEA exercising its strategic planning and leadership roles. It undertook a complete review of everything it inherited from the ILEA, which resulted in: the removal of surplus places in the primary sector; reorganized 16+ provision; a review of special educational needs resulting in the closure of special schools and the opening of units for children with special educational needs in primary schools, and; the amalgamation of the youth service into an area-based Community Education Service.

The overall strategic, cradle-to-grave plan aimed for quality and accessibility in education. SMAD was the part of its implementation which related particularly to the secondary sector. It is a good example because it illustrates all four of the areas which I have defined as the LEA role.

Strategic

You do not need an LEA to invent the idea of school improvement. You do need an LEA to be able to develop the notion of school improvement so that it can operate at a strategic level across the whole of the local community, in a way that schools working together are supporting each other and helping each other improve. You will read in Joan Farrelly's chapter (Chapter 2) the story of the birth of SMAD. It is a story of having an idea and a vision about how the LEA — operating strategically across its schools and with its schools — could act as a catalyst and bring about change and improvement on a much larger scale than any one school on its own could have done. It is a story of leadership and of the proper exercise of the political role of members in making decisions that have a direct impact and which are targeted in a way that supports their political priority. This priority was to believe in the strength and ability of inner-city children and to be determined that those children will not be sold short by accepting anything less than the highest expectations of, and the best possible outcomes for, those children.

Post local management of schools LEAs have to achieve those aims, not through a paternalistic model but through providing a framework and within that framework exercising a quality assurance and monitoring role that delivers public accountability while at the same time helping the schools to develop as institutions. There are tensions in this role, because if an LEA gets it wrong, schools can always opt out. There are particular issues if a school is in difficulty as to what is the correct balance between pressure and support.

Resourcing

Because local management of schools is connected in people's mind with the delegation of the budget to schools, it is easy to make the mistake of believing that post-local management LEAs to not have anything to do with the finances of schools. In fact, they have a key resourcing role. They decide how big a share of the total council budget will go to education. They decide how that will be divided between the non-locally managed schools sector and the rest of the education provision such as community, adult, youth, and nursery school provision. They decide, through the construction of the local management formula, the general principles affecting the distribution of money between schools — in particular the weighting between primary and secondary schools. The resources of the SMAD project is an example of that process in action.

Hammersmith and Fulham was due to make budget cuts in 1992. The 'normal' way of approaching this situation is either by a percentage cut across the board or differential percentages for different services. In Hammersmith and Fulham the approach was different. There was an attempt at zero or baseline budgeting, i.e., building up the budget from first principles, deciding on priorities, and allocating the reduced resources according to those priorities. Education generally was identified as a priority and, within that, improving achievement was the focus. This resulted in growth in three areas of education even though this in turn resulted in greater cuts in other parts of the council. Those growth areas were an expansion in nursery education in the under-fives area, extra staffing in primary schools to focus on literacy and basic skills, and the *Schools Make a Difference* project in secondary schools.

There was a considerable injection of resources to SMAD: £300,000 revenue and £240,000 capital to be shared between the eight schools. Members were clear that although the schools would decide what they spent the money on, it wouldn't just disappear into the LMS 'pot'. Through the 'animateur' (and who else but an LEA could have created that role?), there would be LEA involvement in an overview of the process by which schools, working with the animateur, decided how to spend the money, which was very important and for which rules were laid down. Some overall decisions were made by the LEA at an early stage, e.g., the capital and revenue split. In the last resort there existed an LEA veto over the expenditure. Schools did not regard this as an attempt to undermine LMS. They did not clamour for the money, which was a not inconsiderable sum, to be delegated through the formula. They accepted and supported the fact that it was a specific

LEA initiative and that what went with that was ultimately the Authority having a say about how the money was spent.

Support

The support the LEA gave to the schools through the SMAD project went beyond just the resources as such. The animateur worked four days a week with and in the project schools. As well as coordinating she was advising, coaxing, leading, inspiring, encouraging, supporting, overseeing, developing and stretching the schools. She facilitated schools sharing with each other, which was especially important in the context of open enrolment, league tables and competition. This was key to the success of the project. It held it together. It provided the strategic framework in a very tangible way. Schools gained a great deal of support from the meetings of heads and coordinators — sometimes separately, sometimes together — that were a feature of the way the project developed. The visits to schools in other parts of the country were also an important part of this support organized by the animateur. The LEA publicity machine was also used to support the project by producing leaflets (etc.) promoting and explaining the project. It was hard to explain at first. This was particularly true for members, who were used to making very specific decisions on how money should be spent.

Although they were retaining overall control of the SMAD money, as far as possible, within very broad guidelines, the decisions were left to the schools and even before they could make them, the decision-making process itself was an important and quite a lengthy one. Members at first found this perplexing, wanting to know what exactly SMAD was, what it meant, what the money would be spent on and what the outcomes would be. As director, it was my job to mediate the project with members and give them confidence in the ability of individual schools to use the money in ways that would achieve the council's aims for school improvement. Due to the work done in this area, schools gradually became proud to be part of this LEA initiative and SMAD became a household word.

Monitoring

Hammersmith and Fulham has always taken very seriously its responsibilities for monitoring the quality of education provided in the borough. The basis of the Education Committee's commitment to working in partnership with all its schools and asking them to 'opt in' to the local authority is that, although an LEA can sell its services to the grant maintained (GM) schools, it loses any locus for the quality of education provided there and that is key to the LEA's role.

Pre-Ofsted, Hammersmith and Fulham had its own formal and thorough inspection system which resulted in reports on individual schools going to open committee. It developed systems for monitoring schools outside the formal inspection arrangements. It has made arrangements to meet its statutory responsibilities to monitor how the National Curriculum is taught and to check that assessment arrangements are in place and that local management is being properly handled by governing bodies. It clearly would wish to monitor and evaluate very carefully a specific initiative such as SMAD with the level of resourcing that has been put into it. The project manager monitored carefully what the schools were doing. She worked to the chief inspector who also took a direct interest in the project. As director, I was kept informed and was involved in looking at outcomes of the SMAD work. An external evaluator was appointed to give an objective analysis of success or failure of the project and regular reports were made to Education Committee which culminated in a final evaluation report in January 1995 (see Chapter 6).

I attended the opening of a number of new, flexible learning centres in the schools. I also saw the environmental improvements brought about by the use of some of the capital money and I listened to the heads and coordinators talking enthusiastically about the affect the project has had in the school: I do not think it is wrong to make a subjective judgment that the LEA resources were well invested. My one subjective caveat would be that in any school which is experiencing severe difficulties there is a problem about that school making the best use of any kind of support that the LEA can put in, and this would also be true of the SMAD initiative. However, part of the ethos of the initiative was that it was available to all secondary schools and I would not wish to have been selective.

In conclusion, then, if the LEA role was to have the vision and the imagination and was, willing to back that with resources, the resourcing angle was and should only have been on a pump-priming basis. Like all such projects the aim must be that it is mainstreamed when the money runs out and that the benefits of it are continued after the resourcing has ceased. Again it is too early to make a judgment about whether this will definitely happen. At a residential meeting of the heads and coordinators in the Summer Term 1994 which I attended they were all very clear that they wished the local authority to continue to facilitate developments arising from the project but that they understood that this would now have to be on the basis of the schools paying for the inputs. There can be no greater testimony to a school's commitment to the importance of something, than their willingness to spend their own, very hard pressed budgets on it.

2 The Chief Inspector's View

Joan Farrelly

I write about this project from the point of view that it was only one aspect of my work among many. All of them, I hope, contributed to the gradual improvement in the education offered to the children and adults of the London Borough of Hammersmith and Fulham.

The break up of the Inner London Education Authority (ILEA) in April 1990 brought groups of schools together on a geographical basis which had been largely irrelevant to the previous metropolitan pattern of education. Nowhere was that more evident, or potentially more of a problem, than in Hammersmith and Fulham: eleventh in descending order of size of the thirteen new education authorities, and formed from 60 per cent of the former ILEA Division 1. (ILEA Division was originally formed from the London Boroughs of Hammersmith and Fulham and Chelsea and Kensingston.)

The nine secondary schools we inherited from ILEA comprised virtually all the permutations of organization — voluntary aided girls' (2), voluntary aided boys' (1), voluntary aided mixed (2), county mixed (2), county single sex (1 of each). The closure of one of these schools had already been set for April 1991. (A voluntary aided boys' school in the borough had become grant maintained prior to April 1990.) The performance of the schools was, historically, very varied. In terms of examination results, two were above the national average, one hovered on the average, the rest were below — some concerningly so. Along-side this, and the pattern did not coincide with examination success, the schools were very different in their preparedness for local man-agement of schools (LMS) and in their understanding and practice of development planning. There was little cooperation between the schools and some suspicion: alliances in April 1990 were not particu-larly good within the borough.

Among the dozens of pressing priorities in the months before April 1990, three educational issues recurred and were particularly acute in relation to the secondary sector:

- First, how to establish a shared understanding of school development that incorporated mutual aspirations regardless of previous performance history and the currently increasing competitiveness.
- Second, how to raise professional morale and reduce the effects of the perception prevalent among teachers that they were victims of politically motivated reorganization, locally and nationally.
- Third, how to refocus attention freshly on the entitlement of our inner-city children, raise their achievement, and give expression to the belief that schools can make a difference to the life chances of children.

The idea of a project that would encourage the eight secondary schools to work together along similar lines was conceived during the preparation for takeover in April 1990 — before the embryonic LEA had full evidence of how much such a venture was needed. At that time money was not available. There was no point in starting a project with a sizable group of disparate schools unless the LEA could offer funding that the schools would manage and use as an integral part of their distinctive projects. In 1992 the education department, alongside other council departments, had the opportunity to bid for some one-off growth money from the council. Alongside proposals for nursery expansion, and a Reading Recovery project for the primary sector, the *Schools Make a Difference* (SMAD) project was put forward as two-year venture involving all the secondary schools, operating to a fairly tightly drawn brief (prepared under pressure), and taking its chance among all the other bids across the council. It is to the credit of the elected members of that administration that over the summer 1992 they listened, questioned and were convinced that it was worth backing the eight secondary schools to the tune of £540,000 over two years, as one part of a concerted effort across early years, primary and secondary, to improve standards of achievement.

The Aim

The Education Committee paper of 19 October 1992 set out the proposal in its original form:

Perhaps the biggest single issue in education today is the under-achievement of pupils, particularly in inner-city areas such as

Hammersmith and Fulham. The aim of the *Schools Make a Difference* project is to work with the eight secondary schools to raise the level of attainment, achievement, participation and morale, without adding significantly to the work load of teachers.

The belief system underpinning the project included:

- that good behaviour is a necessary condition for effective learning, and students are effective partners in regulating conduct;
- that students need to believe that school can be a different and relevant experience — to achieve this the 'logic of learning' must be perceivable by students, and adults must work consistently across all aspects of school life to establish relationships with pupils;
- that learning must be challenging and relevant, i.e., students should be able to connect it with the world outside school;
- that students' intellectual, personal, and technical abilities must be recognized, and demands made on them that consistently reflect high expectations of progress and performance.

The methodology envisaged was expressed thus:

- the well-researched features of school effectiveness and school improvement are an appropriate model;
- all outcomes of a plan–do–review approach should be tested against improvements, which must be visible in the classrooms, corridors and the school grounds.

Some initiatives were set out in the original paper for the Education Committee to take place under the aegis of SMAD. These included:

- a mentoring and monitoring service for the senior management teams that would establish the features of effective schools and the senior management contribution to school improvement;
- extended day arrangements providing high quality study facilities after school, based on strong in-school tutorial systems;
- visible improvement to the school environment and other ventures based on pupils', parents', staffs', and governors' involvement;
- resources to help set up effective arrangements for consulting

with students within schools and across the borough. This would feed into all the initiatives that are seeking to involve pupils in an active and positive way in the life of their school;

- resources to encourage each school to choose a different aspect of the curriculum as a model for development — in effect becoming a major resource base for the borough for inservice training.

Any initiatives undertaken within the project were intended to be integral to each school's School Development Plan.

The Project Manager

By the time the project was possible, the inspectorate had been reorganized, twice. Once, because of budget cuts literally days after taking up responsibility. Later, as the implications of LMS (and other funding devolved to schools) was increasing, the LEA was pressured to provide a 'support through monitoring' function, at the expense of the 'support through advice' role. The inspectorate's increased responsibility for monitoring was not easily compatible with the kind of support role required to manage this project. While each school's link inspector was expected to work closely to the project, another kind of person was needed:

> Although the project will be overseen by the Director of Education and the Deputy Director/Chief Inspector, an 'animateur' will be employed on a two-year, fixed-term contract, and will work with the schools on the planned initiatives and provide support and encouragement on a day-to-day basis. The person appointed will clearly have to have the experience and personal qualities to command credibility among the headteachers. (Paper on the Schools Make a Difference Project presented to the Education Committee 19th October 1992)

This description omits to mention the psychological stamina required to handle eight very different schools, to withstand the pressure to cut corners in the processes, and get on with spending the money — to put it somewhat crudely. Fortunately, in Kate Myers the schools found an animateur of rare experience and qualities who, always practical, held firmly to the principle that long-term change, such as that embedded in the project, must be woven into each school's development plan from the beginning.

Before Kate's appointment I had explained the project to the eight headteachers at one of their, now, regular meetings — bonding was beginning! There was a willingness to suspend disbelief, and some enthusiastic recognition that this *was* a genuine chance to improve aspects of their schools' functioning. There was enough goodwill to go forward. Two headteachers selected by the group were part of the appointing process: that gave credibility to the idea that the partnership envisaged with the LEA and with the animateur was more than rhetoric. Indeed, throughout the project, heads were involved in policy decisions about management issues and the deployment of resources.

I became the project manager's line manager and chaired the project's steering group until I retired in April 1994. Consequently I was able to support and monitor the initiative through Kate and liaise with the director and political members as necessary, freeing Kate to get on with the day-to-day work of managing SMAD.

Retrospective commentary

An important purpose of this book is to evaluate the effectiveness of the project, and I am conscious that the intensive activity that characterized the last eight months of the project happened after I retired. I can offer a partial and a personal view of one who, through the project manager, had sometimes a day-to-day, and consistently a week-to-week, line-management contact with SMAD.

In broad terms the project was successful in many aspects, most evidently perhaps in the number of schools who have built features of it into their practice through their School Development Plan. While not detracting from any of the achievement, in the course of the project the emphasis, pace, and outcomes changed to some extent:

- I think it was right to launch the project quickly and without much attention to warnings about getting people 'ready for change'. My observation would be that when people changed, they did so as their understanding developed by taking part in the project activities.
- My belief in the critical influence of the headteacher was reinforced by this project, although the energy generated by the middle managers when given the opportunity to carry initiatives

through was equally arresting. My impression is that, in general, senior management teams as a whole did not develop an understanding of their influence as fully as the original brief intended.

- I realized, during the sixteen months in which I was involved with the project, that I was holding a very firm line on embedding practices in schools' management processes and ethos. I am aware that my demands were seen as tough. My view is that someone has to be a back-stop for the project leader and, on the fundamental principles, has to be unmovable.

- The project schools were more inward looking than I hoped. The original initiatives saw the entire school community being involved. This did not happen fully in any school. Effective schools surely command the support of the wider community by sharing their endeavours as part of a learning society. There is still work to be done between SMAD-type projects and the current Royal Society of Arts (RSA) project with parents. The broader aspect of the project, reaching out from the schools across the borough to reinforce a responsible and committed student voice, was not attempted. I understand why, but as I indicated at the beginning of this chapter, this wider aspect was important to me. Headteachers cannot be expected to have an LEA strategic view, and will only respond to measures that speak to their school's needs. If they do more it is a bonus.

- Linked with the broader aspects, such projects must be watchful that they do not go too easily down a well-trodden research path: replicating results is not a particular virtue in this essentially practical field. The idiosyncrasy of projects, answering legitimate local and political imperatives, should be fostered. In this way, action research will be more responsive to local aspirations and conditions, and will, in its turn, keep the academic research into school improvement/effectiveness replenished.

- If one could have foretold the national educational maelstrom of recent years, such a venture would never have started. As it was, several central government measures impacted upon the project. For example:

    (i) National Curriculum arrangements at Key Stage 3 and Key Stage 4 leached confidence in curriculum development. In the longer term, I predict, the secondary schools in Hammersmith and Fulham will wish to offer each other expertise in an area of study. At the time, however, it was not appropriate, and this strategic development was not attempted.

(ii) Similarly, I think, I did not reflect adequately on the likely 'effect of Ofsted inspections, as against the equally thorough (3-year rolling programme), and public, inspection process of the LEA. We were fully aware that the schools were very different in terms of effectiveness, but politically generated criticism (often along party lines) was unhelpful to at least two of the schools. One point of the SMAD project was to give schools a demonstrably equal chance to improve in ways appropriate to them. I think we now know, what previously was only suspected, that there is a cut off point past which schools in difficulties cannot use 'normal' help to arrest decline and sustain improvement. This issue has a currency that needs addressing nationally, not just by one LEA. I see the processes and intentions of SMAD as appropriate help for schools that are functioning 'normally'.

(iii) In the circumstances, it is proper that recording aspects of the project which went well and very well should be the prerogative of those whose contact extended to the end, and who indeed are still working. My reflections are within that wider quality framework for which I was responsible for five years.

The questions have been asked of me: Would I do it again? Would I do it differently? If circumstances are broadly similar, such as in the current national reorganization of local government, I believe this approach to school improvement continues to have validity. The detail would be different because contemporary constraints and opportunities would be different. However, I think I have learned that such undertakings must have:

- a shared point of view, which will be modified by individual schools;
- some main players, including an animateur, who understand and uphold the importance of process;
- a focus on pupils within the context of the wider school community as a whole;

- some teachers who have enough confidence in their professional expertise and in their moral authority to become the
  active agents of change;
- visible and demonstrable outcomes, some of which must be
  speedy. This is not to underestimate the importance of the
  process through which schools learn to continue to change;
- adequate funding which the schools have to manage together
  as an integral part of the project (any sense of 'throwing money
  at the problem' must be avoided);
- responsibility for the project taken by someone with a strategic
  role within the authority;
- built-in monitoring through which the individuality of an LEA
  project is maintained, but with sufficient links into the national
  school improvement network not to become parochial.

Finally, school improvement is an issue for all schools, however good
they are. LEAs have a vital role in supporting this work. The *Schools
Make a Difference* project was one such attempt to do so — and an
encouraging one.

3 The Project Manager's View

Kate Myers

Setting Up

The information that candidates for the post of project manager or 'animateur' (See Chapters 1 and 2) received included a description of the basic tenets of the *Schools Make a Difference* (SMAD) project based on research on school effectiveness and school improvement. These nine 'guiding principles' were drawn up in consultation with the headteachers. They were that:

1   Students need to believe that schooling can be worthwhile and a relevant experience, and that they understand the logic of learning and receive frequent and specific feedback on their progress. Ways of relating to students should be consistent.

2   Learning must be challenging and relevant. Students should be able to make the connection between learning and the world beyond school and be encouraged to develop their capabilities as responsible, thoughtful and active citizens.

3   Students' intellectual, personal and technical abilities, aptitudes and capabilities are recognized and valued and that challenging demands are made of them which consistently reflect high expectations of progress and performance.

4   Good behaviour is a necessary condition for effective learning; that students are partners in regulating conduct and must take responsibility for their own behaviour; that lessons are well structured and organized, activities are appropriate to the needs of students, and there is a high degree of engagement by the students in the learning process.

5   Parents play a vital role in the education of their children and that ways should be sought to involve them as much as possible in this process.

6   All staff in the schools are involved in, and committed to, the school's development.

7   Schools and the community work together towards a shared vision and that school staff create a professional learning community where members share and learn together.

8   Headteachers have a vital role to play in providing a climate where this can occur.

9   A 'plan, do and review' approach is systematically and rigorously applied. This is central to the project's success.

As well as this list, candidates for the post received suggestions about possible initiatives and information about the resources available. There was a generous budget (revenue: £300,000 over two years; capital: £240,000 over one year), a basic outline of the philosophy of the project, and a deadline. At this stage the budget for the project was set and finite. The duration of SMAD, though, was dependent on how long the money lasted and how long the schools wanted to be involved within the two-year period that the money was available.

No lead-in time had been planned and within this context one of my first tasks when I took up my job as project manager in January 1993, was to propose a structure and ways of operating that were agreeable to the heads and officers and related to the basic tenets of the project.

Appointment of Coordinators

I was well aware of how busy heads are and, although also aware of the importance of their role in all the relevant literature (Sammons, Hillman and Mortimore, 1995), predicted that they would not have the day-to-day time to give to managing a project of the size and scale that was being proposed. The same research literature also emphasized the importance of involving staff in improvement initiatives and I consequently proposed to the heads that each school should appoint a project coordinator who would work in partnership with them.

The coordinators who worked on one of the previous projects in which I was involved (the School Curriculum Development Committee (SCDC) and the Equal Opportunities Commission (EOC) in 1986), did not receive any class contact remission or extra pay for their work, an issue that was picked up by the external evaluators (Jamieson and Tasker, 1986). The SMAD heads therefore agreed that their coordinators should have non-contact time specifically for the project and an incentive allowance. It was also important that this non-contact time should be the same afternoon each week so that when the coordinators attended inset or meetings, disruption to classes would be minimized. It was agreed that until this could happen, i.e., when new timetables were in place, the meetings and inset would be arranged at different times of the week in order to avoid the same classes being covered too frequently. From September 1993 the non-contact time was established as Thursday afternoons which allowed the coordinators to meet together regularly, without causing disruption to classes. (In hindsight it would have been better to arrange for this to happen during a morning as frequently coordinators had to leave inset early to get back for after school meetings.)

Once these decisions were made we agreed that the posts should be openly advertised and interviewed in the normal manner. However, this did mean that the coordinators would not be appointed until the end of the spring term at the earliest, given the time needed to advertise, apply, shortlist and interview — a long time to wait in such a short-term project. Formal interviews were held in seven of the schools with the head, myself and one member of the governing body. Confronted by two good candidates at interview, one of the heads who was managing a split site, decided to appoint both, (one for each building) financing the additional coordinator from the school budget. Only one head decided not to make the appointment this way and she approached a head of department and asked him to take on the work as an additional responsibility.

The Structure

It was agreed that three groups would manage the project. A steering group would be formulated with representatives from other parts of the education service and the community. The heads would together form the strategic management group which would make policy decisions, and the coordinators would meet regularly as a group to discuss and decide day-to-day practice and procedures.

The Steering Group

Initially this group consisted of:

- two representative SMAD heads and coordinators
- a primary head
- a special school head
- a parent governor
- the education officer from the Commission for Racial Equality (CRE)
- the chief inspector
- the lead officer in the Education Department's Research and Statistics section
- the project manager

The intention was that the chief inspector would chair the steering group until members got to know each other and could elect a chair.

The group met four times during the project and at its second meeting devised its remit:

1 To advise and support the project during the implementation and dissemination phase.
2 To distribute information about the project as appropriate.
3 To act as a link between the project and the wider community.
4 To receive the evaluation and contribute to the final report to Education Committee.

Members of this group had considerable difficulties in attending regularly — indeed the parent governor (for personal reasons) was unable to attend after the first meeting but did not resign immediately and was subsequently not replaced until July 1994. One of the coordinators did not receive the relevant information and never attended. One of the SMAD heads resigned his post in December 1993 and the primary head moved to another authority at Easter 1994 — at the same time as the chief inspector retired. Attempts were made to resurrect the group in the last term of the project. A new parent governor and primary head were appointed, the retiring chief inspector was invited to remain on the steering group and the education officer from the CRE agreed to be the chair. Unfortunately at the meeting held in September, 1994, both the new primary representative and the chief inspector were unable to attend. As apologies were received in advance, the final meeting was cancelled and the group never fulfilled its remit.

The idea behind setting up this steering group was to liaise with, take notice of and involve a wider constituency — an idea that seems sound and worthy. The reality of creating a meaningful dialogue in this way is, however, difficult to establish in practice. The issues we faced seem to be comparable with those schools face when trying to set up similar networks. This does not make the idea any less worthy but it does mean that more time and effort need to be spent in persuading the wider community that it is worth their while to be involved — and then ensuring that this is the case.

The Heads' Strategic Management Group

The heads' group met for business and administrative purposes ten times during the project. Although there was already a tradition of the secondary heads meeting it was not often that they were all able to attend. Nor did they normally have any 'outsiders' present at these meetings. (Their formal communication channel with the LEA was through a heads' meeting that involved heads from all phases. The eight secondary heads were obviously outnumbered at this forum and somewhat resentful that they did not have separate access, as secondary heads, to the director except on an *ad hoc* basis when there was a secondary issue to address.)

At the first SMAD meeting in February 1993 they were all present but it was not clear whose meeting it was, whether I was a guest at theirs or they were attending mine. Before my appointment they had nominated two of their number to be the SMAD representatives. These two heads had together devised the interview procedure for the project manager's post and had been members of the interview panel. It was agreed that they should continue to be the SMAD representatives and fulfil that function on the steering group. However, although I proposed that policy decisions could be made with these two colleagues acting as the heads' representatives, the heads were reluctant to surrender this function and decided they would prefer to meet as a whole group regularly with me. This was an important decision because in spite of all the other pressures on their time they decided they wanted firsthand involvement in policy decisions about the project. However, subsequently there was a feeling amongst some of the heads — it became apparent in the interim evaluation — that there had been too many meetings and they were spending too much time on the project (see Chapter 6, 'The Evaluator's View').

The Coordinators' Group

Most of the coordinators were heads of department. Two of them were heads of large curriculum areas and with the addition of their SMAD responsibility they became senior teachers and members of their senior management team. Having prior experience of dealing with whole school issues and direct access to the decision-making process probably made life easier in the first instance for these coordinators. As the external evaluator points out in Chapter 6, the 'learning curve' for some co-ordinators was very steep at the beginning of the project, when it was important to organize a whole school response to the initiative and then cost and produce a Project Plan. The coordinators that had in-school support, particularly from the head or a deputy, found this task considerably less stressful than those that felt they were doing it on their own.

One of the undoubted successes of SMAD was the way the coordinators' group 'gelled' and the consequent support members of the group gave each other. In the climate and reality of open enrolment and the consequent possibility of competing for the same students, it was reassuring to witness the coordinators (and the heads) generously sharing ideas and strategies.

Heads and Coordinators

The evaluators of the SCDC/EOC project already mentioned, pointed out that during that project the heads would have appreciated more support. In that project, the coordinators enjoyed and benefited from regular and high quality inset. This also gave them the opportunity to meet regularly, share news and act as a supportive network for each other. Nothing similar was arranged for the heads who consequently felt increasingly deskilled (Jamieson and Tasker, 1986, p. 7). Additionally the evaluators believed that the most successful schools were those where there was a *partnership* between the head and the coordinator.

> Here the coordinator and the head work together on the project, with the head often taking on a specific research project or other activity. Where it was in operation in the project it proved to be a very powerful vehicle for change. (Jamieson and Tasker, 1986, p. 8)

The SMAD heads were consequently offered the possibility of inset support and the head/coordinator partnership model was actively encouraged. This proved moderately successful though some of the heads, as described in Chapter 5, found some of the joint inset less useful than the sessions mounted specifically for them as a group.

Getting Going

The Budget

Two distinct budgets had been allocated by the members to support SMAD. £240,000 had been earmarked for the capital budget and £300,000 for the revenue. The intention was that the capital budget should be spent on physical improvements to the environment and the revenue should be used to support all other aspects of the project.

One of the first decisions that the heads' strategic management group made was that the capital budget should be divided evenly amongst the eight schools on the basis that neither the size of roll nor other factors made a significant difference to the cost of physical improvements. This group also decided that money from the revenue budget not used for administration purposes and supporting centrally run inset, should be divided amongst the schools according to the local authority's Additional Educational Needs index (AEN). This index is based on size of roll and social deprivation of students. Consequently schools were eligible for significantly different amounts under this budget. It was also agreed that the revenue budget should be subdivided into headings for travel, conferences and inset, use of consultants, extended day and revision centres, student consultation, working with parents, supply cover, and curriculum material. These headings were based on the initial consultation paper on which the project was founded.

The local authority had always made it clear that the SMAD budgets would not be devolved to schools but would 'follow the work'. This enabled stringent monitoring to take place and ensured that the budget was only used for the purpose for which it was intended. However, an unanticipated but probably inevitable outcome was the enormous amount of work that arose from clearing and processing the vast number of invoices that ensued from each school. Spending the money (properly) was much more time-consuming than anyone had anticipated.

Project Plans

At one of the early strategic management group meetings we agreed that schools would put together a project proposal for each of the two budgets and that it would be useful to prepare a common proforma for this purpose. The proforma went through various drafts before it was eventually agreed. The proforma was designed to help schools go through the consultation process and the final version began with questions about the school's development plan and which issues from this plan they had chosen to pursue as part of the project. The purpose of this was to ensure that SMAD was not seen as a bolt-on project but as an opportunity to pursue issues that the schools had already identified as central to their own needs. The proforma then asked for information relating to equal opportunities, other school developments and how and when teaching and support staff, pupils, governors and parents had been consulted about the proposals. The final component required a detailed action plan indicating what resources (human and material) were needed, inset and financial requirements, and a section about plans for monitoring and evaluating success and strategies for dissemination.

At the time this all seemed like a good idea. It was essential that as many stakeholders as possible were involved in drawing up the plans and it was anticipated that the proforma would assist the process. What happened, however, was not quite so straightforward. Some of the heads worked closely with their coordinators, working parties were set up and procedures went through relatively smoothly. However, even in these schools, it all took longer than envisaged and plans were not ready until the beginning of the autumn term (i.e., term three of a six-term project). In other schools, coordinators were left pretty much on their own and those with no similar previous experience found the job of coordinating these proposals more than a little stressful. (See the coordinator's own stories in Chapters 4 and 5.)

Before arriving at a whole school consensus each individual proposal had to be costed, which was essential but extremely time-consuming. The proposals also had to relate to the financial subheadings already described, e.g., conferences, cover, travel and inset. Schools then had to be able to demonstrate how their proposals related to the basic tenets of the project. In my view several proposals did not meet this requirement (e.g., showers for the male staff of one school), and a few 'full and frank' discussions took place. On some occasions, after discussions with coordinators and heads, I was convinced; on others, proposals were resubmitted.

This situation neatly illustrates a tension that I felt throughout the project. On the one hand, I believed in and wanted to encourage school-based decision making and in particular give the schools back a feeling of empowerment and control. On the other hand, I was responsible for a large budget, and had a fairly clear idea what school improvement was and was not about and a very short time-scale to demonstrate success. Almost all these differences were resolved amicably but there is no doubt that on occasions (*albeit* rare) there was some resentment about my interventions. At least one of the heads made it clear that he would much rather have 'taken the money and run' and felt he knew what was appropriate for his school without any outside interference.

What We Did

Strategies

It is important to note that no-one associated with SMAD is making any claims that the intervention strategies used in the project were either unique or should be universally adopted by schools. Many of the strategies were 'borrowed' from schools already successfully using them. They are described below in this spirit. Some of the strategies were planned at the outset of the project (e.g., extended day provision for students, inset for staff), others emerged and evolved during it. These strategies tended to fall into four categories, directly affecting:

- Staff
- Students
- Parents
- Improving the learning environment.

All the schools produced their own final reports and some of the quotations following in this chapter are from these reports.

Directly affecting staff

The heads and coordinators participated in seven joint inset sessions and two residential conferences. Issues addressed at the inset sessions with nationally known facilitators, included working with parents, student behaviour, flexible teaching and learning strategies, the 'Improving Quality of Education for All' project (IQEA), performance indicators, Ofsted's 'Improving Schools', and using 'value added' to measure the school effect. In addition, the heads had two separate inputs, one about school effectiveness and school improvement and the other about managing change in a large commercial organization with a senior organization consultant from Zeneca (formally ICI).

At the first weekend residential conference, which took place in October 1993, six of the schools' senior management teams and the coordinators reflected on progress so far and planned future strategies. The second 24-hour residential conference for heads and coordinators took place in June 1994 with the aim of evaluating progress so far, planning for the final term and planning for post-SMAD.

With support from Dr Louise Stoll at the Institute of Education, London University, a skeleton inset programme on school effectiveness and school improvement was devised for the separate coordinators' inset. They were then invited to identify their needs and a term-by-term 'top-up' programme was added. In addition the coordinators were able have the work they did for the project accredited towards an advance diploma at the Institute. Four of them took advantage of this opportunity.

Visits to 'interesting' schools
Another form of inset was visits to 'interesting' schools around the country. This idea of visiting 'successful' schools was mentioned as a possibility in the original information that went to candidates applying for the project manager's job. There are many definitions of a success-ful school and given that raw league tables and word-of-mouth recom-mendations were the only data available, the alternative definition of 'interesting' schools, was adopted. Finding the schools was more diffi-cult than anticipated (Myers, 1994a) and it was salutary to note that because the information was in the public arena, it would have been much easier to gather a list of 'failing schools' (as they were then known). Ofsted's publications 'Improving Schools' (1994) and the chief inspector's 1993/4 annual report listing fifty-two successful schools, have subsequently been a welcome attempt to publicize and celebrate schools that are doing well. Nevertheless, although this information was not available at the time, using a variety of informal networks a list of 'interesting' schools was eventually produced. The criterion used for selecting these schools was, essentially, improving exam results. The results of several of the schools were not impressive using the raw results published in the league table, however they were all using deliberate strategies to improve these results and were able to demon-strate success in this area.

The SMAD visitors consisted of senior managers (heads, deputies, senior teachers), coordinators and myself. The largest group for any particular visit was ten and the smallest three. Where possible we trav-elled together and the ensuing conversation on the forward and return journeys provided opportunities to discuss educational issues in general and what we had seen in particular. Without exception, host schools were generous — both with their time and the sharing of ideas. They were pleased that the work they were doing was being acknowledged, valued and appreciated and said they found the visits stimulating. We found the visits one of the most beneficial forms of inservice experiences we had undergone and several SMAD initiatives were adopted and adapted from practices we had observed. (It was rumoured of one senior management team in particular that they got increasingly concerned every time their head went on one of these visits because of all the good ideas with which she enthusiastically returned . . .) Visits to other schools were subsequently organized by coordinators for their colleagues. For example over a period of two terms, 45 per cent of the staff at one school visited a school in a nearby authority that had an exemplary flexible learning centre.

School-based inset
In addition to the centrally provided inservice opportunities, coordinators also organized twilight and training day sessions supporting the focus of SMAD in their schools. For several schools the focus of these sessions was supporting the development of flexible teaching and learning. Coordinators reported that these sessions were generally positively received by colleagues with some of them being outstandingly successful.

> That's the best inset I can remember having in this school. (Teacher at Henry Compton School commenting on SMAD inset and quoted in the school's final report.)

Inset for middle and senior managers
At the first residential conference, deputy heads and senior teachers were offered the possibility of a course or inset opportunities being created for them and geared to their own needs. There was little enthusiasm for this however and consequently nothing was arranged. In hindsight I am not sure whether, as project manager, I should have been more assertive, arranged something and 'encouraged' participation. This was another example of the tension between (passively?) responding to perceived needs or (actively?) creating them.

Several months later, some of the heads raised this issue again and asked for something to be organized for middle and possible senior managers. This time two deputies were involved in devising the course in conjunction with the inspectorate and it started with a 24-hour weekend residential in September 1994. Follow-up twilight sessions were planned to run for the academic year (i.e., after SMAD had formally finished) run by the inspectorate. This inset was late in the day for an obvious 'project effect' (see the evaluator's comments in Chapter

6). Nevertheless it responded to the needs of the group, both in terms of content and when it was offered. It may have been more sensible to be more proactive in this area and offer centrally run inset for middle and senior managers at an earlier date. On the other hand, they may not have been 'ready' for this sort of provision. This is a perennial issue for external agents — finding the right balance between meeting needs identified and encouraging 'clients' to realize that they have needs.

Cover

In order to facilitate the development of curriculum materials, visits to other schools and inset, each school had access to money to pay for supply teachers to cover lessons. Achieving the right balance between allowing teachers time to engage in such activities but at the same time ensuring that the disruption to the learning of students is reduced to a minimum, is a perennial problem. Consequently most schools under-spent this budget and negotiated viring it to support other aspects of SMAD.

Burlington Danes school was an exception here and departments were encouraged to put in bids to the coordinator to use this budget to plan and structure their inset in a proactive rather than reactive way. They used this opportunity to visit other schools with good practice, to develop materials and new schemes of work, and to develop resources and strategies for their new flexible learning centre. The school then canvassed the students to see if they had noticed a change in the teaching (see Chapter 5).

St Mark's School instigated a 'critical friends' scheme (see Chapter 6) whereby teachers chose a partner and observed each other in the classroom. Other schools used some of the cover time set aside in the budget to work in departments to develop resources for their flexible learning centres.

The schools also had access to a range of 'project consultants'. This list grew as schools added to it, sharing the names of consultants they had found useful. Indeed, several of the SMAD participants became 'consultants' themselves as they dealt with an increasing amount of requests from other local authorities for speakers about the project.

Directly affecting students

Enhancing learning opportunities

Four of the schools used SMAD to establish flexible learning centres (FLC). These centres provided opportunities for students to do independent research using a variety of audio-visual resources and access to IT facilities including CD-Roms. As well as being open to support teaching during normal lessons, most of the schools arranged for these centres to be open before and after school and during the lunchtime. Several also made the facilities available during half-term breaks and the Easter holidays. Staff were delighted with the response of students to these facilities

> I use the FLC for lots of different things . . . I have recently used the CD-Rom in order to research my Shakespeare project . . . the machine has a large store of information on Shakespeare's life and works and the theatre of his day. I use the FLC most during lesson times, to type up class work, or get a print-out of something. I sometimes use it for doing homework. (Year 8 student at Lady Margaret's, quoted in the school's final report)

Revision centres and coursework clinics
One of the most successful strategies of SMAD proved to be opening the schools in the holidays as study centres. Part of the budget had been earmarked to support such provision and so it was possible to pay teachers a modest sum for organizing and running the sessions. Each school appointed a 'tutor in charge' who was responsible for organization, publicity and evaluation of the scheme.

In the first year of the project, seven of the schools opened up during the Easter holidays to enable students to revise for their forthcoming GSCE in an atmosphere conducive to study, supported by appropriate resources and the availability of their teachers. (Myers, 1994b) This experiment proved so successful that three of the schools decided to offer similar facilities during the October and February half-terms and all the schools opened during the Easter holidays of 1994. (The research and statistics section in the education department undertook a survey of those students who attended and planned to match the results of these students in order to compare them with those of students who did not attend.)

Students were extremely appreciative of the opportunity to come into school to study:

> Gives time to revise in peace and quiet. Help is there if you get stuck on any questions. (Year 11 student, Sacred Heart School)

They gave the following reasons for attending:

- help with particular subjects;
- peace and quiet to work;

- help with coursework;
- help with exam technique and use of special resources.

Students were very grateful for the support they got from their teachers. Comments, such as the following, were not unusual:

> I would like to thank all the teachers for their help and coop-eration. We all really appreciate them giving up their spare time to help us and their helpfulness has given us all a real incentive to try our best in the exams. (Year 11 student, Lady Margaret School)

Staff reported a 'knock-on' effect in the classroom and the delights of teaching students who were highly motivated. Staff also reported that these were not always those students that showed such high levels of motivation during school hours.

> Interestingly, students who found it difficult to be engaged learners under normal classroom arrangements, turned up to attend the coursework clinic during the holidays.

When I visited these centres I was often told by creative arts teach-ers how they were particularly pleased to have the opportunity to work uninterrupted for long sessions. For example, in one music session I visited, students were spending an uninterrupted morning on compos-ing a piece — an opportunity not usually possible during the normal school day. In addition, students with learning difficulties and students whose first language is not English frequently mentioned how useful it was to have extra support from their teachers.

Students also reported that parents were delighted with the provi-sion:

> They were shocked that I was willing to come into school during the holidays but they were pleased with me. (Year 11 student, Lady Margaret School)

Although the centres were organized primarily for Year 11 stu-dents, several of the schools reported that younger students appeared too. None of the younger students were turned away. A total of 391 students (51.6 per cent of Year 11) attended the revision centres on one or more occasion. At Sacred Heart, 85.6 per cent of the exam students attended. At Henry Compton, 67.1 per cent of their Year 11 cohort attended at least once. Overall the pupils who attended the revision classes had an average GCSE performance score of 35.7 points compared with an average performance score for those who did not attend of 25.6 points. The lowest impact occurred in the two schools in the borough that already had a tradition of excellent examination results and the highest was in the schools where raw results were below the national average. At Henry Compton school, for example, the average score for students who attended was 28.9 points compared with 12.9 points for those who did not attend (a difference equivalent to one grade 'B' and two grades 'C' per pupil).

Using the London Reading Test as the prior achievement measure, the Education Department's Research and Statistics section were also able to demonstrate that, regardless of their ability, students who attended the centres achieved better results. However, as Keith Pocklinton points out in Chapter 6, these results need to be treated with great caution: although we had anecdotal evidence from teachers that it was not only the students who demonstrated motivation during school that turned up to these centres, it is likely that the vast majority of those that attended were the more motivated students and this would make a significant contribution to the results. We cannot conclude, therefore, that attendance at these centres guarantees higher examination results but there is substantial evidence which demonstrates that students benefited from attending.

We learned a number of important points from running these centres:

- There is a need for such provision. Many of the students have nowhere quiet and appropriate at home for uninterrupted study. This is likely to be particularly pertinent to inner-city students.
- The morning sessions are most effective.
- Pre-planning and publicizing provision is important so that students and their parents know exactly what is being offered each session.
- It is likely that, resources permitting, many younger students would also appreciate and benefit from some sort of enrichment and extension provision in the school holidays.

But there is an issue about asking overworked (and indeed undervalued and underpaid) teachers to take on additional work in their holidays. Their concerns need to be listened to seriously and addressed. In particular:

- Teachers should be paid an appropriate rate for participation.
- Only volunteers should be used (we had no problem recruiting

teachers for the SMAD centres — in fact in one school we had too many volunteers).

Indeed, a perfectly adequate centre can be run with a small number of teachers each of whom need attend for only one session. For example, each subject could be offered for only one half day. Our survey demonstrated that many students do not have adequate facilities in which to study at home. Even those who have their own bedrooms said that they were frequently interrupted by other siblings and home was not a conducive place to study. School students need resources (human and material) to help them complete coursework and to give them confidence and support to revise. For many of them, their only access to this is in their schools.

Extended day provision
Another part of the budget was earmarked to support extended day provision. Schools decided to offer homework, enrichment, and extension facilities after school. Although it was possible to pay teachers (again a modest sum) for running these sessions, some of the schools thought it would be iniquitous to do so since they already had a tradition of teachers running after school and Saturday activities, unpaid, in their own time. These schools were also concerned about what would happen when the funding ceased. They therefore decided to use the funding to buy equipment and resources for the sessions. Other schools paid teachers. We tried to establish whether the provision was more successful when teachers were paid and consequently the provision was on a more formal setting, but could find no pattern. Not surprisingly the success (measured by range of provision, attendance and duration) depended much more on individual circumstances and, in particular, individual teachers.

There was some tension (discussed in more detail in 'The Evaluator's View', Chapter 6) about running purely extra-curricular type clubs (e.g., calligraphy, photography and mural clubs) and running curriculum extension and support activities. My view was that both should be available but, at the very least (for the reasons discussed under the section on revision centres), each school should provide a homework club on as many nights a week as possible. According to the evaluator, some teachers perceived this (alongside comments from their own senior managers) as pressure to offer only academically related clubs.

In one of the schools (see Chapter 4), students made it clear that they were only interested in the extra-curricular provision. This is another tension that needs to be addressed in schools. Many teachers enjoy sharing their personal enthusiasms with 'volunteer' students. The 'knock-on' effects of these relationships in the classroom is well known to anyone who has run such clubs or participated in school journeys. Indeed this is backed up by research.

> Teacher–pupil relationships can be enhanced out of the class-room. British studies of secondary schools have found that when there were shared out-of-school activities between teachers and pupils (Rutter *et al.*, 1979; Smith and Tomlinson, 1990) and where pupils felt able to consult their teachers about personal problems (Rutter *et al.*, 1979), there were positive effects on outcomes. (Sammons *et al.*, 1995, p. 21)

However this needs to be considered alongside the issue of student attainment. I am not suggesting that schools are or should be only about examination results but examination results are the passport to the future for many of our students. We consequently have a duty to ensure they have the best possible opportunities to achieve whilst they are at school. For many, as discussed above, opportunities are not available elsewhere: curriculum extension and support is an important aspect of this provision.

Generally, students were very appreciative of the extended day offer. Some of the schools surveyed their students to discover their views about this provision. The following quotations are taken from Fulham Cross students:

Why did you attend the extended day?

- Because I was having difficulties with my French, so I regularly attended and I feel it has helped me enorm-ously as I have now been entered for an early French GCSE.
- Because homework club gives me peace and quiet and resources.
- Because I wanted to improve my work.

What did you enjoy about the club you attended?

- I like feeling a part of a group of people. The home-work club is peaceful and I get more work done than at home. You can ask for help from the teachers which is good.
- Because everyone there needed help and you didn't

feel so pressurized. You get more individual help. And
there were lots of resources to help you.
- Everything.

Do you think extended day activities are important or worthwhile?

- I think they are worthwhile because they give students
a chance to learn and do things they can't do in the
school day or at home.
- Yes I do think it's worthwhile because I want to improve my work.
- I think they are very important and worthwhile because they give students the chance to enjoy something
or like me, catch up.

Improving literacy skills

Several of the schools (St Mark's, Henry Compton, Sacred Heart, The
Hammersmith) intended to improve literacy skills and encourage reading through the auspices of the project. At St Mark's school the concept
was not just to support the students with literacy problems but to enrich the reading of the able pupils too (see Chapter 5). St Mark's and
Henry Compton also established class libraries for the lower school.

It soon became clear that when offered appropriate materials,
pupils were enthusiastic and literally grabbed at the books.
(Henry Compton School, quoted in the school's final report)

These two schools also established silent reading lessons. St Mark's and
The Hammersmith trained older students to work with younger ones.
Henry Compton school reported an increase in students reading books
(from 15 per cent to 40 per cent in 4 months — figures taken from a
headcount in assembly) and an improvement in National Curriculum
attainment records.

. . . after 9 months, of those pupils who were assessed as level
1 and who subsequently benefited from the Support Programme, just over 50 per cent had reached level 2 or above
and were able to read independently and to express and explain preferences.

St Mark's School reported that of the students identified as having
particular needs in Years 8 and 9, a number of them increased their
reading age as a result of the project, several by more than one chrono-
logical year.

At the Hammersmith School, the target group was fifteen Year 7 students who had reading ages below 7. The programme included 25 minutes daily intervention centred around reading, writing and spelling in small groups of three during tutorial periods. According to the school, results showed that all students increased their reading age by at least 1.25 years. One student increased his reading age by 2.9 years and two others did so by 2.5 years.

Mentoring and target setting

At the beginning of the project I researched several schemes that arranged mentoring support for students with Adults Other than Teachers (AOTs). Some of the coordinators were enthusiastic about adopting such programmes but, in the end, the amount of work involved (identifying and training mentors, organizing police checks, etc.) defeated us all. However the SMAD visitors observed some effective internal mentoring schemes on our visits to 'interesting schools' where concern about the progress of individual students led to establishing mentoring systems for these students. Fulham Cross School decided to introduce such a scheme and members of the senior management team became individual mentors to Year 8 students. This support system was work-focused and students agreed targets at each meeting which were reviewed at the following meeting. This scheme proved highly popular with parents:

> She is much more aware of the importance of homework and classwork.

> I think the mentoring my daughter is receiving is very good as the girls have a chance to talk about a problem and their mentor can check if their work is up to date. (Quotes from the school's final report)

The scheme has now been extended to include older students at Fulham Cross. At one of the coordinators' meetings the coordinator from Fulham Cross described their mentoring scheme. This sharing of strategies was one of several examples where initiatives tried out in one of the schools was subsequently introduced at others.

Journals

Two schools, The Hammersmith School and Fulham Cross, decided to use their SMAD budget, to help students improve their organizational skills by introducing user-friendly, custom-made journals. At Fulham

Cross, pupils were encouraged to set themselves targets and their target-setting sheets were kept in their journal. This gave teachers the chance to see individual targets and encourage the girls to meet them. Both schools found the introduction of these journals useful and decided to continue this initiative when funding from the project ceased.

Improving student morale: Consulting and involving students
The research discussed in the 'Prologue' (Sammons *et al.*, 1995), demonstrates the importance of student involvement in their school and their learning.

> A common finding of effective schools research is that there can be quite substantial gains in effectiveness when the self-esteem of pupils is raised, when they have an active role in the life of the school, and when they are given a share of responsibility for their own learning. (Sammons *et al.*, 1995, p. 20)

We therefore tried to ensure that where possible and appropriate, students were involved in SMAD. Schools either established school councils or used existing ones in order to consult students about the capital bid and improving their learning environment.

> At the inception of the project a student council did not exist within the school . . . student enthusiasm [for this initiative] remained undiminished . . . attendance remained 100 per cent. (Henry Compton School, final report)

Although it put a considerable pressure on the coordinators, the time factor involved in the capital budget (i.e., the budget was only available for one financial year) did mean that the students actually saw and benefited from the results of the consultation procedures.

> The school council has been quite good at getting things done that improve the school. When it started and we were asked to say what we thought would most improve our ability to learn if we had £25,000, I never thought something like the Learning Centre would arrive so quickly. This is good because it showed that the school listened to what the students had to say. (Year 11 student, Henry Compton School)

Several of the schools involved the students in the detail of the capital bid, e.g., choosing specified items.

I enjoyed helping with the SMAD project. I did a lot of work on the common room — things like measuring the area, helping to sort out what to buy and trying to get the rules together from the two rooms. (Year 11 student, Burlington Danes School)

Burlington Danes School then canvassed the students' views on the effects of the improvements to the learning environment and found that 40 per cent felt that their behaviour had improved because of the changes (e.g., carpeting in classrooms, corridors and stairways). (See Chapter 5 for more details of Burlington Danes students' views). Students' views were also sought on a variety of other issues throughout the project, e.g., homework, the revision centres and extended day provision.

Seven of the schools participated in the Keele University survey about students' perceptions of school life. One school, against my advice, decided not to engage in this activity, mainly because the coordinator was planning to conduct his own survey. Unfortunately, for a variety of reasons, this survey was never completed. His school's absence from the exercise meant an incomplete data base. This was an issue not only for the school concerned, but also for all the others as a composite picture of students' views from those local authority schools represented, was put together by the researchers at Keele and compared with their national data base of at the time — 7000 responses (see figure 3.1). This sort of

Figure 3.1: Students' perceptions of school life: A comparison of SMAD students' responses with the Keele University data base

Question	Positive Response (%)	
	SMAD students	Keele University's national data base
• Do you have a positive relationship with your school?	63	59
• Do you think that you attend a good school?	61	73
• Are most of your teachers respected?	37	38
• Is the discipline good at your school?	64	71
• Are you encouraged at school?	83	82
• Are you praised for good work?	83	81
• Are your schoolbooks marked regularly?	51	69
• Do your parents think its important that you do well at school?	97	97
• Do your parents expect you to get good exam results?	92	89
• Is your work important to you?	94	93
• Do you work as hard as you can?	80	78

frustration, however, is probably inevitable if decisions are really made by negotiation rather than dictat. The interesting issue is at what point the 'purseholder' waves 'ownership' and starts making decrees.

The responses from boys and older students tended to be more negative than those from girls and younger students. Schools each received an individual breakdown of the views of their own students and there are obviously a variety of issues for them to pursue. Schools did not administer the survey until near the end of the project so it was not possible to use it for pre- and post-test purposes. However, some of them intend to try it again next year to see if their actions have resulted in a shift in students' views.

Improving student morale: celebration days

One of the aims of SMAD was to improve student morale. Having heard about a very successful 'celebrating achievement' event instigated at one of the 'interesting schools' we visited, that managed to involve the whole school community, two of the schools decided to 'borrow' this idea. St Mark's School and The Hammersmith School both decided to mount catalyst events to encourage an achievement culture. Both schools celebrated 'Black Achievement'.

> This was the first time ever that the school had hosted an evening which not only paid tribute to famous and historical Black people, but which gave an opportunity for our own Black community of students, staff and parents to celebrate with the whole community their own skills, abilities and talents. (The Hammersmith School)

One of the coordinators from St Mark's attended the celebration at The Hammersmith School. St Mark's subsequently mounted their own celebration. Chris Eubank (boxer), Paul Williams (footballer), and Howard Anthony (ex-pupil and an East Enders star) were all guests. St Mark's school followed this by organizing a day celebrating 'Women's Achievement'.

> The emphasis was much less on celebrities but on skills and the contribution made by women in the past, present and future. (St Mark's School; see Chapter 5 for more details)

Both schools felt the events had successfully involved the wider community by helping students identify with successful role models, and had helped to increase students' self-esteem and expectations.

Strategies directly affecting parents

The literature on school effectiveness emphasizes the importance of sound home–school links. Involving parents in the life of the school, however, is notoriously difficult to achieve in the secondary sector. Nevertheless several of the schools attempted to work in this area, with varying degrees of success, and at the end of the project all of them feel there is still a long way to go. Examples of strategies designed to involve parents included:

i) Sacred Heart — Homelink programme designed to involve Year 7 parents in the reading progress of their daughters.

ii) Fulham Cross — Parents in Partnership (PIPs) aimed at encouraging parents into the school to assist with improving literacy skills by listening to pupils read.

iii) The Hammersmith School — Responding to the publicity in the media that followed the Ofsted report, several meetings were organized for parents; a home–school links network was established; and a parents' room created.

Involving parents was probably the least successful aspect of SMAD. Although there is plenty of evidence that demonstrates the importance of this issue (Sammons *et al.*, 1995) most of the studies relate to the primary rather than the secondary sector. Two issues seem to be important here. Firstly, parents of secondary age pupils may find it more difficult to get into schools for a variety of reasons, e.g., the school is more likely to be further away from the home than the primary school (this is particularly true of SMAD schools as most of them were either voluntary aided or single sex — only two drew most of their pupils from the neighbourhood catchment area); parents may have other commitments (for example, where work is available); mothers who stay at home with primary age pupils are more likely to return to work as their children get older, and as the children get older they may be less keen to see their parents on 'their' territory. Secondly, it is important to be aware that just because parents are unable or unwilling to visit the school, it does not mean that they are not interested in their child's education. In fact the evidence is to the contrary. The Keele survey on students, described above, asked them whether their parents considered it important for them to do well at school. An overwhelming 97 per cent responded positively. Further, 92 per cent said their parents expected them to get good examination results and 83 per cent of students said that parents try to help them with their homework. We consequently need to find ways of supporting parents to help their children at home.

Strategies aimed at improving the learning environment

At the outset of SMAD, members had allocated a large proportion of the budget towards capital improvements in the schools. Furthermore, this part of the budget had to be spent within one financial year. Although this put tremendous pressure on the coordinators and the planning and operational section within the department, it also proved very useful and morale-raising as all those involved in the consultation phase saw very quickly the results of this process.

The Rutter study, 'Fifteen Thousand Hours', (1979) found 'a signifi-cant association between good pupil behaviour and good maintenance of decorations and care of the building generally'. Other studies have demonstrated the importance of students' motivation and self-esteem. SMAD attempted to link these two research findings by involving the students in discussions about how their learning environment could be improved. The consultation process itself was found to be valuable by some of the schools:

> It is clear to see that the capital bid has had a large impact on the school in terms of raising a whole community approach to the environment. (Burlington Danes School)

Four of the schools (Sacred Heart, Hurlingham and Chelsea, Lady Margaret and Henry Compton) decided to use this aspect of the budget to establish flexible learning centres. Three other schools managed to use other budgets to provide similar facilities and so there was a joint focus on training staff and students to use these centres as part of a deliberate strategy to broaden teaching and learning strategies (see Chapter 4). Other schools decided to:

- Improve IT facilities (St Mark's, Henry Compton)
- Establish tutorial libraries (St Mark's, Henry Compton, The Hammersmith)
- Carpet and curtain classrooms, corridors and stairways (Burlington Danes, St Mark's, Hurlingham and Chelsea)
- Establish study and social areas for students (Lady Margaret, The Hammersmith, Burlington Danes)
- Establish a multicultural archive (Burlington Danes)
- Improve student toilet facilities (The Hammersmith)
- Improve and extend display facilities (Fulham Cross, The Hammersmith, Burlington Danes)
- Improve students' locker facilities (Fulham Cross)
- Improve playground facilities — picnic benches, litter bins,

plants (Fulham Cross, Burlington Danes, Hurlingham and Chelsea)

- Improve entrances and corridors (Henry Compton, The Hammersmith, Hurlingham and Chelsea)

Although there were considerable pressures on all those involved to implement this phase of SMAD within the time-scale involved the results of these new facilities not only raised morale but also had a direct impact on many of the improvement strategies introduced by the schools.

Issues Arising

Duration of SMAD

Research studies have indicated that change takes time:

> Above all, educational change is a dynamic process involving interacting variables over time . . . (Fullan, 1991, p. 67)

One thing not available to SMAD, though, was a lot of time. The short-term nature of the project (and its uncertain length), meant there were inevitable tensions about giving the 'stakeholders' enough time to consult and reflect before decisions had to be made and action was taken. This is an issue discussed by the external evaluator in Chapter 6.

'Volunteer' Schools

As described earlier in this chapter, all the secondary schools in the borough were invited to participate in the project and they all decided to do so — hence they were all 'volunteers'. Two points arise from this. Firstly, it is difficult to envisage any school not wanting to participate when such a generous budget was available. This is not to criticize schools but to be realistic about the fact that not all heads had a commitment to the ways of working that were advocated. One head, for example, expressed considerable cynicism about any attempts to encourage collegiality and participation. As this process of working was fundamental to the basic tenets of the project, there were occasions when considerable tensions arose. It is comparatively easy to work as a facilitator with schools that are doing reasonably well and who think you can help them and want to work with you — it is more challenging when one or more of these factors is absent! Secondly, although the heads had agreed to participate in SMAD, not all of them had consulted either their senior management teams or the rest of the staff. A considerable number of those who subsequently found themselves involved in the project, had not taken part in the original decision to join. There was consequently some understandable resistance (at least initially) from those who felt no 'ownership' of SMAD. In many cases this situation was ameliorated as the people concerned became involved.

The Tension Between Pressure and Support

Michael Fullan (1991) has discussed the importance of, and interaction between, pressure and support in the change process:

> Successful change projects always include elements of both pressure and support. Pressure without support leads to resistance and alienation; support without pressure leads to drift or waste of resources. (p. 91)

As the external facilitator I had to try and judge when and how to interweave this process in dealing with individuals and the various groups and institutions with which I was working. Support was delivered in the form of individual face-to-face meetings, phone calls, group meetings and inset. Pressure was mainly delivered through time deadlines that (in my view) were agreed, and which I tried to 'persuade' the various stakeholders to keep to. I attempted to keep a reasonable balance between the two, but there were times when some of the coordinators felt there was too much pressure and not enough support. (See the external evaluator's discussion of this issue in Chapter 6.)

There were undoubtedly incidences when I got the balance wrong (some of them have been discussed earlier) and intervened and should not have, or did not intervene and should have. It is often a judgment that is difficult to make especially when made in the context of other pressures being wielded on all the stakeholders — both personal and professional. School improvement projects do not exist in a vacuum. People have babies, breakdowns, operations, end relationships and suffer bereavements. (All of these important life-events affected key stakeholders during the project.) Managing the appropriate professional response is sensitive and easy to get wrong. Furthermore, I was aware that however much I wanted to encourage a participative approach and wanted SMAD to be an empowering experience for the schools, I controlled (subject to approval from my line-manager) the purse-strings. In the end, she who controls the purse-strings has a lot of power . . . This issue became particularly relevant with regard to the production and then the monitoring of Project Plans.

Managing the Budget

There is no doubt that such a generous budget encouraged schools to participate in SMAD and provided the possibility for radical change in schools. Other studies have highlighted the importance of extra resources for such projects (Stoll, Harrington and Myers, 1995).

> Add-on resources are clearly needed for improvement. No new resources, little change. (Louis and Miles, 1990, p. 261)

For once, schools were being asked to make changes and were properly resourced for doing so. However, there was a down-side to this too. Firstly, I thought it was important that the money was only used to support the project and not to resource other needs schools may have had (however genuine). The money consequently followed the work. What I did not anticipate was the enormous amount of work involved in clearing what seemed like thousands of invoices from all the schools. Secondly, managing the budget proved to be very time-consuming for the coordinators too — at times there were dangers that SMAD was becoming just about using the budget not about school improvement. (This problem decreased in the second year once the capital budget had been spent.) Thirdly, large sums of public money were involved: accountability as to how this money was spent was therefore crucial. We tried to keep the bureaucracy as simple as possible but nevertheless some of the schools complained that there was too much. The schools that involved the school administrator early on in the project and where coordinators were well supported by the head or a deputy, found the whole process of managing the budget less stressful than those where this did not happen.

Instability and Inner-city Schools

For reasons explained earlier, there was a considerable emphasis put on the importance of the partnership between the heads and the co-ordinators (the former with the power to allow things to happen, the latter with the time, energy and enthusiasm to get things to happen). Within the first year of SMAD, two of the heads had left the local authority. During the next year another head retired, two key deputies and one of the coordinators left, and the deputy director (who had been instrumental in initiating SMAD and a vital support during its early stages) retired.

Given the importance of the leadership role of the head (and deputies) in the school effectiveness and improvement literature, this turnover of key personnel had profound implications for the project. The staff in three of the schools where the heads left, at the very least faced uncertainty about their own future. Two of the schools experienced acting heads before final appointments were made — not an easy situation in which to encourage planning and development. In addition, this level of turnover caused continuity and induction problems for the project. Although the acting heads and the three new substantive heads were extremely supportive of SMAD, they had not been part of the original discussions, had not participated in the inset or group visits and, because Project Plans had already been formulated, to a large extent were joining a *fait accompli*. In addition, one of the heads joined a school that was soon deemed 'requiring special measures' following an Ofsted inspection and another joined one that had just 'passed' their inspection following a critical report during the pilot inspections. Consequently both these heads had fairly urgent and immediate agendas to which to attend.

External Pressures and Other Agendas — Ofsted

As discussed above, during the project four of the schools experienced Ofsted inspections, three of them during Ofsted's first year. (One of these schools was also inspected as a pilot school in the summer term of 1993 and so experienced two Ofsted inspections during SMAD). Ofsted's remit was to inspect a large proportion of 'schools causing concern to HMI' (Ofsted's *Update, Fifth Issue*, September 1993, p. 5) during its first year. It is likely that the three SMAD schools fell into this category — an important indicator of HMI's view of the state of these schools — *before* the project started.

Of particular relevance to SMAD, was that once schools were notified of an inspection they (understandably) found little time to do anything else apart from preparation for the inspection before it took place and production of the action plan following the inspection. 'Development paralysis' seemed to occur. This had serious implications for a short-term project such as SMAD. (This reaction may diminish as schools face the second cycle of inspections with a reduced 'Framework' and are more used to the procedures. If not, it highlights a serious weakness in the system.)

There were particular consequences for the two schools deemed as 'requiring special measures'. One immediate consequence was the attendant publicity, both national and local — for example, the headline 'Is this the worst school in Britain?' on a double-page spread in the *Mail on Sunday*, 20th March 1994, referred to a leaked report of an impending letter to The Hammersmith School from the Secretary of State informing them that they had failed their inspection.

'State of Readiness'

It was anticipated that the SMAD outcomes would be different in every school. This was largely because schools had produced their Project Plans based on their School Development Plan and therefore although there were many common themes, the plans and expected outcomes were individual to each school. However, there were also other differences between the schools, some of which had significance for the outcomes of the project. Many of the contextual differences have been mentioned above and most are discussed in detail by the evaluator in Chapter 6 (e.g., turnover of key staff, Ofsted inspections, experience of coordinators, support of head).

Not surprisingly, schools responded differently to SMAD. Some were able to use the project to support important change needs already identified by the staff and the project properly became integrated with other initiatives such as TVEI (Technical and Vocational Education initiative) and became a mainstream initiative in these schools (this did, however, cause some evaluation problems as it was extremely difficult to then disentangle a 'project effect'). In other schools, particularly one of the troubled schools, there were too many other urgent and immediate issues that the school had to address before they could concentrate on areas of development. In effect, some schools were in a 'state of readiness' to take on board the necessity for change (in some cases even welcome it). They had the capacity to plan and implement the desired change, according to their own needs. They were able to use the external support available to help them do what they wanted to do. Others, in some cases struggling with day-to-day survival, found it extremely difficult to fully utilize the support when faced with so many serious and immediate problems. There were no adequate maintenance structures in place — a prerequisite for developmental work.

I am not suggesting that SMAD had an adverse effect in any school.

Indeed there were some positive outcomes experienced even in the school that was the most troubled during the project. For example, the students that attended the Easter revision centre in this school (58 out of a cohort of 119) achieved an average GCSE performance score 13.9 points higher than their classmates who did not attend. What I am suggesting is that long-term developmental work is incredibly difficult in a situation where short-term, intensive care, may be more appropriate.

Replicability and Transferability

SMAD was not established with the intention of replicating it anywhere else. (See the 'Prologue' for a fuller discussion of this issue.) Indeed, the underlying emphasis on supporting schools to identify and then work on their individual needs, makes the issue of replicability redundant. However, much has been learned about the process of managing change and it is possible that some of these processes could be transferred, adopted and adapted elsewhere.

Life after SMAD

SMAD was always envisaged as a pump-priming project that would last no more than two years. However, one of the problems with such initiatives is that when the project has finished — and after the funding, enthusiasm, and development work is over — key people leave and other priorities emerge for those left facing the day-to-day reality of the chalk-face. These issues were addressed at the last residential conference in discussion with the Director of Education and then pursued during the final term of SMAD. There was a strong feeling among all those involved that much of the work associated with SMAD should and would continue. In the final report for Education Committee (presented January 1995), I wrote:

The schools intend to:

- continue many of the strategies instigated by the project using their own finances e.g., Revision Centres, Extended Day, student consultation, use of journals, mentoring, tutorial libraries and the critical friends scheme;
- where possible, fund coordinators' non-contact time for the rest of the academic year to enable them to continue working on school improvement issues;

- support regular meetings of the coordinators (organized and managed by themselves) to help sustain the momentum once the project has formally finished.

The local authority intends to:

- offer support to schools through the inspectorate
- facilitate regular meetings of the heads with the director to address issues of school improvement
- continue to run the course for middle managers started under SMAD
- monitor the long-term effects of the project through the inspectorate and the Research and Statistics section
- respond to requests for inservice on this theme.

Patrick Leeson, acting chief inspector in Hammersmith and Fulham, takes up these points in the 'Epilogue'.

References

FULLAN, M. (1991) *The New Meaning of Educational Change* Cassell, London.

JAMIESON, I. and TASKER, M. (1986) *Final Evaluation Report of the SCDC/EOC Equal Opportunities in Education Development Pilot Project in the London Borough of Merton*, Manchester, EOC.

LOUIS, K.S. and MILES, M.B. (1990) *Improving the Urban High School: What Works and Why*, New York, Teachers College Press.

MYERS, K. (1994a) 'Admiring Glances', *TES*, 24 June.

MYERS K. (1994b) 'Pay-off from Holiday Work', *TES*, 30 September.

OFSTED (1994) *Improving Schools*, London, HMSO.

OFSTED (1995) *The Annual Report of Her Majesty's Chief Inspector of Schools: Part 1 Standards and Quality in Education 1993/4*, London, HMSO.

SAMMONS, P., HILLMAN, J. and MORTIMORE, P. (1995) 'Key characteristics of effective schools. A review of school effectiveness research.' A report by the Institute of Education, University of London, for the Office for Standards in Education.

STOLL, L., HARRINGTON, J. and MYERS, K. 'Two British school effectiveness and school improvement action projects.' Paper presented to International Congress on School Effectiveness and Improvement, Leewarden, The Netherlands, January 1995.

RUTTER, M., MAUGHAN, B., MORTIMORE, P. and OUSTON, J. (1979) *Fifteen Thousand Hours: Secondary Schools and their Effects on Children*, London, Open Books.

4   A School's View — Burlington Danes School

Sue Gregory (coordinator) and David Lees (deputy head)

The Deputy Head's Tale

But al be that he was a philosophre.
Yet hadde he but litel gold in cofre;
. . .
And gladly wolde he lerne and gladly teche.
(Geoffrey Chaucer, *The Canterbury Tales*, 'General Prologue')

How We Began

In the beginning was the acronym . . .
(New Testament, Gospel according to John, Ch. 1, v 1)

The first detailed idea I got about the *Schools Make a Difference* project (SMAD) was from Kate Myers, the project manager, when she came to talk to the senior management team (SMT) of the school.

I was not happy after that meeting. My first reactions were sceptical and hostile. I had become very weary and cynical about the almost daily DFE circulars and the sort of initiative to which we had become accustomed: in return for spending days filling in a seventeen-page bid form and attending six planning meetings, someone would give us 87p towards setting up a major project to introduce macramé across the curriculum. (The money, of course, to be spent from the school's LMS budget and then claimed back with more interminable forms, phone calls, loss of paperwork and tempers, and a time lapse of eight months.)

It is worth reporting this, I think, because it was based on a misconception of the purpose of SMAD, and of its set-up, and illustrates clearly what SMAD *isn't*. I thought that it was yet another acronymed initiative, with its own agenda, offering schools money to do things which they didn't want to do. I also assumed, wrongly, that there would be a fairly meagre amount of money available. The reverse turned out to be true, and this is what I think is SMAD's great strength. In fact:

1   The money was there to support the school's *own* development. *We* set the agenda, and were given a lot of help in achieving what we wanted to do. SMAD recognized that schools can best identify their own priorities, and set out to support them in addressing those, rather than imposing yet more from outside.

2   There was a significant budget: enough to make a genuine difference, and to allow bold and interesting things to happen. We had access to two budgets — capital for improving the learning environment, and revenue for improving everything else. The capital budget was divided evenly amongst the schools and we were each allocated £28,000. The revenue was apportioned according to the Additional Educational Needs Index and since we had the second highest in the borough our share of this over the two years was £19,500. (See Chapter 3 for more details about these budgets.)

3   Clear conditions and criteria were laid out. These were very helpful in the management of the project. I did not agree with some of the conditions agreed by the heads (for example, the ring fencing of a large sum for revision centres) but this is only to be expected in a borough-wide project. Overall it was excellent. I thought that it was important to show good grace and to go along with the bits with which I was not so happy. I once heard Ed Koch, the ex-mayor of New York, quoted as saying, 'If you agree with me on seven issues out of twelve, then back me. If you agree with me on twelve out of twelve, see a psychiatrist.' This is good advice.

4   There was very good support and management from the centre. Kate's commitment and capability were important factors in the success of the project here.

The first task for the SMT was to choose the focus for the project in the school. This was relatively easy at Burlington Danes. We had wanted for some time to give a real boost to a review of teaching styles and the introduction of more flexible learning and differentiation. This was already in the school development plan. We also knew that our project coordinator, Sue Gregory, had the enthusiasm and ability to do the job. SMAD was the tool we needed to bring together our school aims, a talented leader who was committed to those aims, and the money really to do something about it. We allocated the revenue bid to this.

The capital bid was similarly obvious to us. Improving the environment has been a priority for a long time. Again, SMAD gave us the means to move ahead with things that we already wanted to do.

The Deputy Head's Role

I will make her an help meet for her . . .
(Genesis, Old Testament, Ch. 2, v xviii)

My role was that of line-manager for the project coordinator, Sue Gregory. This is a role of support and supervision. It went well for a number of reasons:

1 We had a clear structure to our relationship including regular meetings about twice per half term, with a calendar fixed well in advance. At these meetings we would review progress and discuss successes and difficulties. I could listen sympathetically, advise and encourage, and also keep senior management and governors informed about progress.

2 I was well informed by the project coordinator in the school. This is critical. Sue kept me up to date on things by sending me copies of minutes, bids, reports etc. etc., so that problems that needed my help were dealt with speedily, and when we met we could use the time to *discuss.*

3 Sue's administration and leadership were first class. This made the management a pleasure, and also meant that I had the confidence to let her get on with the job.

4 I was fully behind the aims of the project, and went to a number of visits, inset sessions and meetings of those involved in the borough. More of this later, but its importance here is that I knew and approved not only of the activities and processes within the school, but also of the wider aims and philosophy driving the project.

5 The clear and active commitment of the senior management team, via me, gave the project real weight in the school, and helped to prevent it being seen as another little piece of tinkering around the edges. As it happened, we had a change of headteacher in September 1994. It was important for the project that there was a member of senior management other than the

head who could keep continuity and momentum, and who could inform and enthuse the new head.

Why the Project Worked

She's so fine . . .'
('He's so Fine', The Chiffons, words and music R. Mack 1993)

I have referred already to the set-up and significant budget of the project, both of which were essential to success. Three other things stand out as essentials to real success in a project like this:

1   First-rate personnel. Sue in the school and Kate in the borough had the vision, drive and ability with administration to keep the project on the move. Crucially, they also had the ability to bring people along with them, and the strength to absorb the hostility and lack of cooperation that were sometimes directed at them.
2   Collaborative working with other schools and colleagues. The ideas, solidarity and encouragement that this generated among those most directly involved kept the project alive and exciting throughout.
3   Luck. Although perhaps not critical, luck is important. My stroke of luck was that Sue's car was stolen. This meant that she travelled to and from school with the head of science for several weeks, during which conversations along these lines seemed to take place:

> *Head of Science*: So what *is* all this stuff about flexible learning, anyway?
> *Sue*: Well, it's . . .

I think this did more for the project in the science department than all of our formal inset sessions.

Influence on Management

Well please don't ask me what's on my mind
I'm a little mixed up, but I feel fine . . .
(Elvis Presley, *All Shook Up*)

I learned a lot during the project — much of it from working with and talking to colleagues. More later about how important this was. Much of what I learned on the inset and visits we undertook was a reinforcement of what I already believed. The best bits really challenged my assumptions, clarified my thinking and give me practical ways of pursuing the aims of the project.

The visit to two Shropshire schools was immensely valuable. Spending a significant amount of time in other schools and speaking with staff and students is always very interesting. We saw two schools whose results had been dramatically improved by their respective heads. It was the contrast in their styles that I found most useful in helping me to reflect on my own management style. I wrote at the time:

> It was very interesting to see two heads with very different management styles approaching a similar problem: an underachieving school with low expectations by staff and pupils and some behaviour problems. The common theme seemed to be a focus on achievement. This was done very specifically in both schools . . . No messing about and very effective . . . In addition, in both schools a wider sense of ownership, pleasant and purposeful environment and other essential infrastructure to achievement was developed . . .

Outcomes

A lot of the useful outcome was my own mulling and reflecting on what we saw, some of which I've outlined. Specifically;

1 I'm in much more of a position to direct SMAD in directions which will be useful to the school.
2 I have a range of ideas for improving student achievement, some of which will be implementable within the SMAD project.
3 I have some clear ideas about how to use our exam results to guide the school.
4 I'm much more enthusiastic about the possibilities of the project. (And I was quite enthusiastic to start with.)
5 I've made some good contacts with people in other schools . . .
6 I shall be the butt of jacuzzi jokes throughout the borough for the forseeable future.

(May 93)

There were several inservice sessions throughout the project led by excellent people who, like all the best inset of my experience, didn't so much tell me what to do as cause me to think. Of course, they gave me lots of good, practical ideas to try, but their real value was in wrenching my thinking out of familiar ways and along new and interesting lines. These have quietly influenced the way I do things: planning, target setting, monitoring progress, and so on.

Where Are We Now?

And some fell upon stony places . . .
(New Testament, Gospel according to Matthew, Ch. 13, v iii)

There is no doubt that the project has moved us on greatly as a school. The environmental improvements have had a profound effect on behaviour and upon the general atmosphere. In many curriculum areas the work on differentiation has improved teaching and learning greatly. The most receptive areas have made huge strides, because they saw SMAD as a real opportunity to get on with what they wanted to do. It is also true that other areas have not made good use of the project, and we continue to cajole, support and direct them to keep at it. Ultimately, of course, what makes the difference between excellent and mediocre practice are the hearts and intellects of those involved. Even SMAD has not found a simple way of changing those quickly and profoundly. What it has done is to allow good practice to flourish, and to provide management with some tools to help it to germinate in more hostile environments.

Keeping It Going

An object continues in a state of rest . . . unless acted upon by a force.
(Sir Isaac Newton, *First Law of Motion*)

We want to make sure that the work begun in the project will carry on in the school. This means an investment of time and money. We have funded Sue's salary increment from the LMS budget, and have also allocated LMS money for development, revision classes and so on. This will necessarily be on a smaller scale than before, but we are in a much better position than we were two years ago, and I am hopeful that the work will continue almost undiminished.

We also have other important legacies from the project. Not least are carpets, picnic benches, litter bins and noticeboards. We also have a much more active school council, many motivated and committed staff and improved management. These are to be cherished, and I am confident that they will continue.

Final Thoughts . . .

Let's work together . . .
('Let's Work Together', Canned Heat, words and music W. Harrison, 1970)

Two essential underlying things have come through to me very strongly from the project. The first is that school improvement *works*. Keeping school improvement at the forefront of what you do, keeping your goals clearly in mind and overtly working at them is effective. There were dark days during the project when nothing seemed to be going right and I wondered what I was bothering for. I am reminded of the great physicist, Neils Bohr, who kept a horseshoe over his door. One of his distinguished colleagues noticed and said, 'Surely you don't believe in that stuff, do you Neils?' Bohr replied, 'No, of course not — but I'm told it works even if you don't believe in it.' The same applies to school improvement.

The second thing is the importance of collegiality. The project brought together all of the LEA secondary schools in the borough. The flow of ideas, support and solidarity were very important ingredients for success, and demonstrated very clearly the value of schools working together. This is in stark contrast to the Department for Education's view of how to improve schools. I am grateful to Andy Hamilton for his permission to print a paraphrase of one of his *Million Pound Radio Show* sketches, which sums this view up neatly.

> (The scene is a newsroom. The newscaster is interviewing the Minister for Aviation)
>
> *Interviewer*: Minister, is it true that you plan to abolish Air Traffic Control in Britain?
>
> *Minister*: Yes, indeed. We want to remove these pettifogging restrictions, and allow pilots to make bold decisions about where to fly and land.
>
> *Interviewer*: But surely pilots will crash!
>
> *Minister*: Mr Day, the *bad* pilots will crash, and this will improve the quality of flying as a whole . . .

A very important principle of SMAD, and of school improvement generally, is that schools working together rather than in suspicious competition is a very effective tool for improvement. We plan to continue to work with colleagues in the borough and throughout the country towards a common goal: to improve our schools, and to give the students in them the best possible education.

The Coordinator's Story

Getting Going

I applied for the post of SMAD coordinator in March 1993. The job description, as I saw it, was for someone to develop and coordinate flexible learning across the school. I was interested in this area so I applied. I remember at the interview Kate Myers saying to me, 'You seem to know a lot about flexible learning but what about the other areas of the project?' I got the job and then wondered what were the other areas that Kate had referred to!

After Easter 1993 things started to happen — the first coordinator's meeting at Cambridge House (the Education Department) was a nerve-racking affair. I arrived last and managed to squash my self in the last available chair and then looked around the room at the other coordinators. Why did everyone look so much more confident about their new role than I did? I later found out nearly everyone else had felt equally unsure of themselves. Everyone introduced themselves and the meeting started. Kate outlined the key aims of the project and then started explaining about the two budgets we could bid for — capital and revenue — and how they were the vehicle to start the change process. There was a lot of talk about 'school improvement' which I thought was a simple term for getting things changed and making them better — I didn't realize at that time there was a whole department at the Institute of Education working on 'School Improvement and School Effectiveness' and that you could get a PhD in it. I was starting to wonder if I was actually in the right place — no one had mentioned flexible learning.

We were very fortunate in the fact that a lot of money was provided by the LEA to support this project. Papers were circulated around the group showing the breakdown of monies under both the capital and the revenue budgets. It seemed like a lot of money — in fact it was a lot of money! £28,000 for the capital and then approximately £19,500 for the revenue. Kate made it quite clear that the monies were not interchangable and the capital budget had to be spent within the financial year. The headteachers had agreed the headings. Fine — but what did capital and revenue mean? I later discovered that capital referred to improvements in the physical structure of the school or environmental improvements, whilst revenue was the term used to explain spending that would directly or indirectly affect students level of achievement and self-esteem. Areas such as inset for staff on different teaching methods which could help raise achievement and revision clinics for students could come under this category. Money could not be vired within the revenue budget — this rigid structure was later to be broken down somewhat, but at the time my mind was racing through ways in which the school could spend every single penny in each section to good use.

The coordinators decided that it would be a good idea to have a common proforma for producing a Project Plan. Draft proformas were produced and we were asked to comment on them. No one had anything to say apart from 'Yes, they look OK'. If the others were like me at that stage, we were still trying to come to grips with the sums of money involved and all the things we were supposed to do, in the time we had been allocated. Anyway, no one had ever gone through with me what a success indicator was — I was later to work out that there are quantitative and qualitative indicators and the qualitative ones are sometimes of more use, even if you can't draw a nice graph with them!

Back at School

I went to a senior management meeting and explained what I had found out at the first coordinators meeting. There was a tight time deadline on the capital budget as we had to consult widely before producing a Project Plan and then commission and complete any building works within the financial year. Was it really worth it? I think so because the capital bid money allowed the school to do things that had been on its development plan for some time. As a school we were able to respond rather than react to this opportunity. One key issue was that the school would need to set up a whole school council so that student views could be canvassed for the capital bid. This was one of the key criteria laid down in the consultation procedure. Meg Conway accepted the role of coordinator of the school council and arranged meetings straight away.

The next thing that was needed was a 'SMAD Working Party'. I remembered a colleague's phrase 'death by working parties' and wondered how I would get on. I asked for volunteers — not just teaching staff, the request went out to support staff as well. Colleagues responded in a very positive way and I got twelve volunteers. This group included the headteacher's personal assistant and the technology technician. In addition, two of the school keeping staff said they would like to be involved but could not attend the meetings.

The reason I asked for volunteers was to avoid the image that here was another initiative that required a standard working party. I decided that volunteers would be better and I was confident in my ability to encourage a wide range of people. The next thing was how to keep them all interested — at the meetings we had refreshments, quite a novelty, and the promise that things were going to happen quickly. Furthermore, everyones' views were valued and respected. The working party drew up a list of improvements required around the school and these were circulated amongst staff and students. Amendments were made and additions included. We ended up with a shopping list that could run into tens of thousands of pounds, which we had to prune somehow. This was a similar problem to that faced by colleagues in other schools. The key point was that the school community was involved from the start.

There was a general consensus amongst both staff and students that carpets would make the place a far nicer place in which to work and study. However, one colleague remarked it was a waste of time and the money should be going into books and resources for the students, not carpets. A couple of the cleaning staff made it quite clear that they were unhappy about the introduction of the carpets since the chewing gum, which the students dropped on the floor with amazing regularity, would be very difficult to get off and would result in shabby carpets — very quickly. It was important to address these issues — I spoke to the colleague about the book situation and another member of the working party checked out the conditions of service for the cleaning staff once the carpets had been laid. It was important that issues such as these were not just ignored, since the project affected the whole school community. The book problem was partially resolved by releasing money from the TVEI budget for flexible learning materials, although the point of principle remained. The chewing gum problem has not really been resolved. A suggestion from the school keeper was an industrial strength cleaner and time allocated to clean the carpets properly. This has yet to happen because of the age old problem of there not being enough money to afford to pay for this extra cleaning time. The key point is that even though we did not have the money to solve the problem, the school improvement literature does point to the fact the concept of involvement is vital, even if you cannot always solve the difficulty posed.

The other areas identified for development were a multicultural archive — to reflect the variety of different backgrounds represented in the school, lots of display boards and photo frames, a study area for Year 11 students, and some external improvements selected by students in Years 7–10.

The students' views were essential at this point, not simply since they had to have a say because we had to demonstrate their involvement in our project bid, but because it is their school. We wanted to involve students at as many levels of the decision-making process as possible within the school. We knew that change imposed by a small group would not result in real development unless there is ownership.

Writing the Capital Bid

Armed with all the information, I set about trying to construct the Project Plan. I had several difficulties to overcome — not least the fact that the proforma did not lend itself easily to my size of handwriting and I did not, at that point, have easy access to a computer. I had to show on the proforma what our success criteria and performance indicators were and I still was not sure what the terms meant. I had lots of information gathered up by the working party but was not sure how I was going to get everything done by the deadline date — and still maintain my workload as head of humanities. I ended up taking the handwritten bid to the deputy head's home at about 9pm on the evening before the critical meeting where the heads would be examining the different bids. It was a success — the first bid to be accepted by the borough without amendment — the hard work had been worth it. The project was actually under way . . .

Students and Staff Working Together — What We Did with the Capital Bid

The multicultural archive — proposed by Charlene Manning, Denise Ailara, and Carmen Campbell (Year 7 students) with the assistance of Jenny Argante, manager of the learning resource centre

Several students new to the school in Year 7 made regular trips to our newly opened learning resource centre looking for different multicultural resources for homework set in art and design and history. There were some materials but not really enough to reflect the make-up of the school. Three of them talked about this problem with Jenny Argante, the manager of the learning resource centre, and together they came up with the idea for a multicultural archive to reflect the multicultural make-up of the school.

Aware that students were being consulted about money available to support SMAD they discussed the kind of things they would want in an archive and how much it would cost. They needed support from other students for their idea and bravely decided to address the Year 7 assembly. This went very well and though they considered talking to older students in other assemblies they decided it would take too much courage! They got around the problem by devising and circulating a questionnaire which asked whether other students would use such a resource and what kind of objects, posters, etc., they would like to see in an archive. They received a very positive response. This is how the students defined a multicultural archive.

The Multicultural archive is a collection of books and other resources, such as artefacts (art and crafts, costumes, musical instruments, household utensils, etc.) kept together in one place.

The items will be for short-term borrowing or classroom use only, and have been chosen to illustrate aspects of all the different cultures represented within the school.

Many students completed the questionnaires and the information gained from this exercise helped inform the final proposal. The students also contacted different companies to see if they would like to donate posters, artefacts, and so on, and in several cases the girls were successful.

In order to formulate the final bid they visited a Black cultural archive established in Brixton. This was the report by Denise Ailara, Year 7:

Visit to Black Cultural Archive Centre — Brixton — On Friday 16th July 1993. Charlene, Carmen, Ms Argante and I went to visit the Black Cultural Archive in Brixton.

When we arrived we were met by Cheryl Levy who showed us around the archive and gave us great information on setting up our own multicultural archive. After we looked around and took notes we went downstairs to Timbukto.

Timbukto is a place where they sell books, clothes and artefacts. We had a great time picking books and posters. Ms Levy told us some interesting facts, for instance, how long black people have been in Britain, since the early 16th century. She also told us about how black people are represented in positive and negative images.

Going to the Black Cultural Archive was very inspiring to us and has given us many ideas for our multicultural archive.

Year 11 study area/common room

Some Year 11 students decided they wanted to establish a combined study area/common room. Three of them devised a questionnaire to find out when and how the other students in the year would use a common room / study area set up by the governors and SMAD. The questionnaire was completed by 62 per cent of the year and the results indicated that the idea was very popular. Once the idea had been accepted, they set about organizing it.

> I enjoyed helping with the SMAD project. I did a lot of work on the common room — things like measuring the area, helping to sort out what to buy and trying to get the rules together from the two rooms.
> Sometimes it was annoying because other students in Year 11 wanted things but weren't prepared to put any effort in.
> I designed some SMAD* certificates for people who had worked on the project so they could put them in their NRA [National Record of Achievement]. We also gave one to Ms Gregory for her help. (Ross Hemson, Year 11 student)

> (*These SMAD certificates explained how individuals had contributed to the project.)

The picnic bench saga

Students from all year groups decided they would like picnic benches outside. It sounded so easy. You order a few benches, they arrive, are assembled, are put in place and students sit on them — but nothing was as simple as that. The students chose some benches and organized getting them ordered. The benches arrived in boxes and someone stole one! Not a good start . . . Other difficulties included the sites the students particularly wanted, which turned out to be health and safety risks — the fire engines would not be able to get past in the event of a fire. A member of the PE department pointed out that if the benches were near the pavilion they would probably be used as foot scrapers, by students coming off the field on a muddy day. The school keeper pointed out to me that if the benches were not physically fixed to the ground they probably would not be around that long. One had gone already and we could not afford to lose any more. Money would have to be spent on fixing the benches to the ground — in fact it cost at least as much to assemble and fix them to the ground as it did to buy the them. However, they are now used constantly by the students — but the new bins that the students requested don't seem to receive quite the same attention!

'It's a nice idea [picnic benches] but in this area of London things get vandalized' — school keeper talking to me after an intruder had come on to the school site and damaged two of the benches. I suppose the next step will be how we will try to stop this kind of mindless damage.

Other improvements to the learning environment

The SMAD project also paid for whiteboards in the mathematics rooms and these have proved to be a success with both staff and students: students are able to see the work clearly; and staff and students are not covered in chalk dust each time the board is cleaned. There are now a lot more noticeboards in use around the building, because of the SMAD project, with a wide variety of students' work on display. The question of lockers was raised by the school council at the time of the capital bid and money was originally earmarked for this — however, when the governors made money available to the school council, the students decided to spend the SMAD money on picture frames and litter bins and to use the governors' money on lockers. The issue of the lockers is still being followed by the school council as a priority.

Changing the Environment

Student responses to the 'improved' environment

All the way through the project we attempted to evaluate what was happening and wherever possible tried to get a student perspective. We had to evaluate as we went along to check that we were on the right track: if not, then we could change things.

In order to evaluate the students' attitudes Alice Faucher, a member of the working party, designed a questionnaire to find out the students' responses to the changes in the environment. With the help of some students — in particular two members of Year 9 Sushma Patel and Terry Janotti — approximately 20 per cent of Years 8–11 were surveyed in September 1993. (There was no point in asking the new

Year 7 about their views on the changes since they were not present before the SMAD improvements to the environment.)

The questionnaire asked the students whether they thought the classroom environment had improved and whether this had had an affect on their behaviour (see figures 4.1 and 4.2).

Figure 4.1: 20 per cent of Year 8 students were asked whether they thought the classroom environment had improved and whether this had affected their behaviour

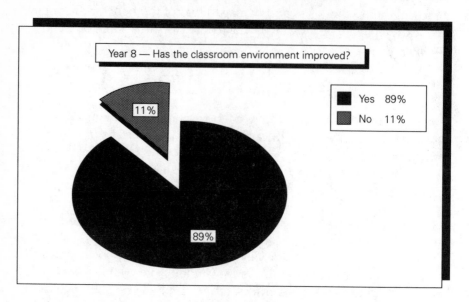

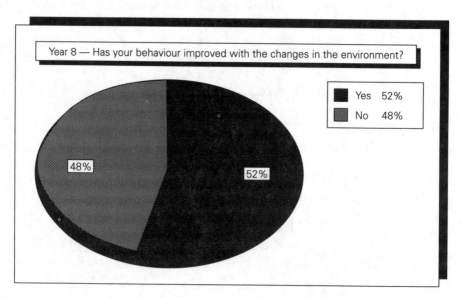

Figure 4.2: 20 per cent of Year 11 students were asked whether they thought the classroom environment had improved and whether this had affected their behaviour

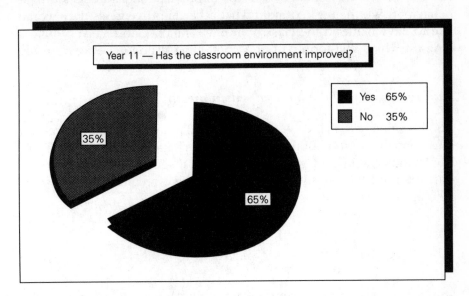

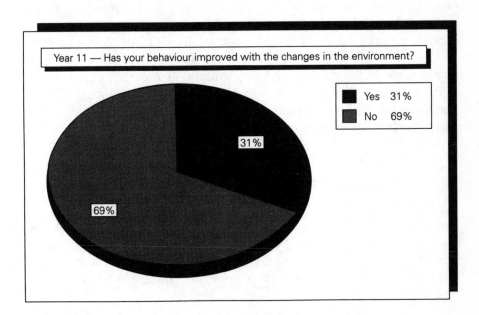

More of the older students were aware of the improvements but more of the younger students felt the improvements had effected their behaviour. We then asked them what other improvements they would like to have made in the classroom environment and received quite a long list which will form part of a continuing dialogue between us all.

Staff responses to the 'improved' environment

Another member of the working party, Alaistair Bennett, designed a questionnaire to find out the difference the changes in the environment had made to staff and where we needed to go next. 51 per cent of staff returned the questionnaire and again we received very positive responses.

The Capital Bid — A Conclusion

So what have been the lasting impact of the changes brought about by the capital bid? The new Year 11 are now using the common room and developing its identity further. The school council has developed to explore a wider range of issues, such as the changes to the uniform and bullying. The display boards are regularly up-dated and students take a pride in their work. The multicultural archive has expanded its range of 'stock'. Perhaps the most important development is the fact that the whole school community worked together on a single project and achieved some measurable success.

Putting It into Practice and Making It Real

Linked with our school development plan, the main focus of our revenue bid (completed early September 1994) was the development of flexible teaching and learning styles; the establishment of after school extension and enrichment classes; and the establishment of holiday time revision centres and coursework clinics.

As well as involving the students as much as possible in the capital bid we were keen to discover their views on school life in general and so with most of the other schools in SMAD decided to use some of our revenue funds to participate in the Keele University survey of student views and perceptions of school.

Focus 1 – Flexible teaching and learning

The SMAD working party organized a one day staff inset programme to raise staff awareness of flexible teaching and learning styles and allow departmental teams to evaluate where they were at and where they wanted to go, in terms of teaching and learning development. This proved to be a successful day with the staff-led sessions being particularly highly rated in the evaluation returns.

Money was also made available from the SMAD budget to allow colleagues off site to visit other schools with good practice or to develop materials/new schemes of work on site for the students.

All departments could take advantage of these opportunities by filling in a bid sheet — it was not a case of first come first served so teams could plan and structure their inset in a proactive rather than reactive way. However, nor was the money just dished out — the teams had to 'bid' for it and unsatisfactory ones were sent back for amendment. There was obviously potential for disagreement with this method but as it turned out all colleagues felt the system was fair and therefore went along with it.

We were encouraged from the start of the project to link SMAD initiatives with other school developments and at this point the curriculum deputy delegated money from the TVEI budget which we could allocate alongside the SMAD monies for the promotion of flexible teaching strategies. From the chart below, it is possible to see the variety of different ways in which departments chose to use the money.

Team	Date	Focus of the Development
RE	January 1994	A flexible learning unit to deliver GCSE coursework
Maths	January 1994	Design a revision pack for Year 11 students — aim to raise achievement in the C/D bulge.
Art & Design	February 1994	Design a unit based on 'Relief' working at the V & A. Aim to raise the D bulge and motivate widest range of students.
English	May 1994	Development of an independent reading policy at KS 3.
Modern Foreign Languages	May 1994	To produce differentiated materials using existing schemes of work for Year 7 & 9.

Science	July 1994	Design a scheme of work on 'Space' for Year 9 KS 3 and Year 10–11 KS 4. Aim to introduce more flexible approaches to learning.
Technology	July 1994	Develop a teaching pack on how to work in constructional material in CDT.
Humanities	July 1994	Design an integrated scheme of work on the local area which has a skills-based emphasis.
Music & Drama	November 1994	To train staff to use the new sound equipment so they can then train students to use the facilities in their own learning.
Diploma of Vocational Education	November 1994	Develop the action planning sheets by students on case work studies and rewrite some casework studies.

What the students thought about some of the developments
We wanted to know what students thought about teaching and learning styles — what they find useful and effective and why? As staff adopted new strategies and introduced new materials we asked the students their views.

Art and design 'The work was more interesting because we saw a wider range of work.' (Year 10 boy)

RE 'I found the new work more interesting because it had more life to it.' (Year 11 boy)

Humanities 'I like this topic because we've been on a trip round the local area and we went to lots of places.' (Year 7 girl)

It is clear from the range of answers provided that students had noticed a change in the teaching and learning styles. However, we realized that not all students want to or were able to take responsibility for their own learning. This an issue we are now addressing.

Research links — working with an MPhil student
Through the inset organized for coordinators, we became increasingly aware of the research available on school effectiveness and school

improvement. When we were approached about whether we would be interested in working with an MPhil student on her research project into student self-evaluation and its impact on student learning we immediately agreed as her focus seemed to have a direct bearing on our focus of teaching and learning styles. Over a period of approximately three months, the student worked directly with three teachers and different groups of students. Other members of staff and a variety of parents were also interviewed at a Year 10 parents' evening to find out their views on learning and student self-evaluation.

The school has been promised a copy of the case study once it has been written up. We intend to discuss and take heed of the findings. We are starting to see ourselves as a 'learning community'.

Focus 2 – Enrichment and extension classes, and holiday provision

From September 1993 we embarked on a programme of after school enrichment and extension classes funded by SMAD. Students were asked to suggest clubs they would like to see running, and staff were invited to run the clubs and get paid for it! The enrichment classes included: photography, calligraphy, mural club, music and songwriting, netball, reading club and the culture club (whose focus was to examine multiracial issues through a variety of different approaches including film visits, food tasting, presentations, debates and speakers). Extension classes were run in food and technology, modern foreign languages, religious education, history, English, mathematics and year group homework clubs.

We decided to keep data to help in the evaluation and found a range of interesting facts including, for example, that few Afro-Caribbean students attended the Year 10 and 11 extension classes. A much wider range of students attended the art and design club whilst the culture club appealed to a wide ethnic and age range. Clubs such as the calligraphy club were very popular with younger students, particularly girls. One thing was quite clear, enrichment classes (where students could learn something new) were a lot more popular than extension classes (where students could get help with their homework). This information raises important questions and will help inform our future planning.

Student Views on the clubs and extension provision

'They are good because you can get extra help from the teachers.' (Year 7 boy)

'I liked learning about France and tasting the cheeses.' (Year 7 girl)

'It's good to be able to use the computers after school — I can get my work finished.' (Year 11 boy)

'I won the calligraphy prize and got a nice pen.' (Year 7 boy)

'I think its important that they [the clubs] carry on because I like the small classes.' (Year 8 girl)

'The clubs are fun and I learn a lot.' (Year 10 girl)

Coursework clinics and 1994 exam results

As part of SMAD we also ran a three-day coursework clinic in the October half-term of 1993 and a one-day clinic in the February half-term of 1994. In addition, the school provided a revision centre for examination candidates in the Easter holidays 1993 and 1994. All these were well attended. The LEA Research and Statistics section were then able to match the results of the students who attended the centre with those that did not (see figure 4.3).

Figure 4.3: Average GCSE performance score at Burlington Danes School by whether or not pupils attended revision classes in 1994

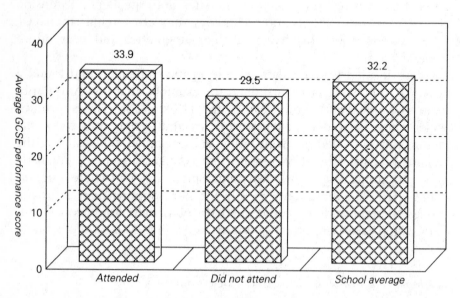

This analysis includes data on 134 pupils (80 attended, 54 did not)
Pupils who were not entered for any exams are excluded
Produced by Education Dept R & S

It is clear that this holiday provision is of great help to the students. There was a marked improvement in the exam success of those attending the revision centres over those of similar ability who didn't attend. The undoubted success of these centres has encouraged the governors to continue funding them after SMAD has formally finished.

Flexible Teaching and Learning and the Extended Day Programme Linked Together in the Keele University Survey

In June 1994, Burlington Danes took part in the Keele University survey on students' attitudes to school and work. The results of approximately 20 per cent of the school Year 7–11 were collated and compared with the average of the 5000+ students that have participated in the research to date throughout Britain.

The reason for participating in the survey was to check students' attitudes to school and use it as benchmark to build on positive responses and examine negative responses to see how as an institution we can address any areas to 'improve pupil commitment, expectation and achievement. The climate of the school needs to be one where pupils feel it is legitimate to achieve.' (Keele University)

A sample of students were selected at random, according to advice offered from Keele, and were supervised whilst doing the questionnaire. Most students said they enjoyed completing the questionnaire, though a few thought it was a waste of time. The information was widely circulated to staff eliciting a mixed response. Comments have included things such as:

'Very useful — a summary of the areas of concern and strategies for improvement should be part of the follow up.'

'Very valuable info — should be lodged in the staff development library.'

'Overall the results don't surprise me. I think many of the students do feel dissatisfied with the school and that we can try and do something about it — e.g., end of year school trips, a much better reward system, more evaluation and time to work and develop the curriculum, more support for teachers to take trips — both day and residential visits.'

'Students misconception — lack of realism re ability is a problem I feel.'

The survey alerted us to the deterioration of students' attitudes to school in Year 8 — the fact that many students didn't feel that they were listened to and therefore the need for staff to listen more to students. However, most students did feel that both their parents and the school were concerned about them as people. We now need to find ways of addressing the issues raised in the survey.

So what didn't we do that we set out to do?

One area that we originally intended to address was involving parents through the development of workshops. However, due to pressures on staff time we were unable to get these off the ground. Some of our original number-crunching evaluation plans also proved a bit too ambitious or not so relevant when we came to consider them.

Keeping It Going

Much of SMAD is now embedded in to the school, however we realize that it is important to keep the process evolving if it is to have longer term impact on the school. Burlington Danes will be maintaining the initiative through the following methods.

1   The governors have decided to continue funding my post for a further two terms so that I can further develop both the after school and holiday provision as well as the differentiated teaching and learning styles.
2   The enrichment, extension provision and coursework clinics, and revision centres are to be financially supported by the school governors.
3   The Keele survey has been analysed in some detail by several staff and the head. Some of the comments will be used to follow up key areas — such as rewards, the relationship between students and teachers, working positively and steadily on the development of teaching and learning styles and methods, the type and quantity of homework, the implementation of the anti-bullying policy, continue working on and developing the school attendance policy and practice, and addressing the issues raised by Year 8.
4   Further inset and support for flexible teaching and learning is planned.
5   Staff development, particularly for middle management, will

continue to develop from the courses provided by SMAD through use of GEST (Grant for Education Support and Training) funding.

6   The SMAD coordinators will continue to meet after the project ends.

In Conclusion

As the project coordinator, I would say that the school has successfully used the resources provided by the project to move forward the areas outlined by David Lees in the introduction to this chapter. We have a lot of information about the school that we didn't have before, we have learnt a lot about school improvement and the way in which areas can be successfully developed, and there is a programme to continue with the work. There have been regular and successful inset and business sessions for both heads and coordinators which have established a network between the schools that we all plan to continue post-SMAD. On a personal level, as a coordinator I have learnt a great deal in a short space of time, which I hope is reflected in this chapter.

Acknowledgments

Thanks are due to all staff and students who have contributed to this report and, in particular, David Lees for his support and allowing me the space to get on with running the project; and to the working party — Alice Faucher, Alaistair Bennett, Carmel Cameron and Maggie Tyler — for all their hard work done on a voluntary basis.

5 A School's View — St Mark's School

Donna Drake (coordinator) and Lesley Mortimer (headteacher) with Mike Dick (coordinator)

The Head's Story

The School

St Mark's is a voluntary aided, mixed, Church of England comprehensive school. For the duration of the SMAD project it had 500+ students on roll of whom almost 60 per cent were from ethnic minority backgrounds, mainly African Caribbean and West African. It is very much an inner-city school with the considerable disadvantage of being situated on two sites over a mile apart. Years 7 and 8 are housed in a Victorian triple-decker building which still has no indoor toilets for students. Years 9, 10 and 11 are located in leafy surroundings on the edge of Bishop's Park in a building constructed in 1954 to accommodate the entire school, at that time a boy's secondary school.

St Mark's has a long and illustrious history. It was founded in Chelsea in 1843 as a 'practising school' for St Mark's Church of England Training College. After the move to Fulham, girls were admitted in 1962 and it subsequently became a fully comprehensive school. Throughout the 1980s, academic standards declined and the 'plant' — particularly the lower school building — received little in the way of modernization or upgrading. The managerial problems associated with running a school of two distant and disparate halves loomed ever larger and the governing body made a number of serious and costly but ultimately abortive attempts to bring the school together on the Bishop's Park site.

In 1990, with a change of headteacher and chair of governors, efforts were resumed to seek a solution to the divided campus. A neighbouring borough who had long harboured the wish to establish a Church of England secondary school within its boundaries offered a disused building. The local Diocesan Board of Education eagerly espoused our cause. Unhappily the first attempt to transfer the school

— lock, stock and barrel — failed on a point of law. At the time of the birth pangs of the SMAD project, however, legislation was being prepared to permit the move to take place. It was against this background — which from the very start posed a moral and financial dilemma for Hammersmith and Fulham in terms of the implementation of the project in St Mark's if it were to remove 'midstream' to another borough — that I threw in my lot with my colleague heads and in March 1993 attended the first of many inservice meetings aimed at spreading the gospel of school effectiveness.

The Heads

The eight secondary headteachers in Hammersmith and Fulham were well known to one another prior to the onset of the project. Three of us, as heads of Anglican schools, were also used to meeting together outside the borough arena, at diocesan conferences and the like. So there was no need for introductory sessions in order to become better acquainted and certainly no feeling of trepidation or disinclination at the prospect of attending management or training sessions with one another over the next two years. Although heads of very different schools with very different problems, we were united in wishing to raise levels of student achievement and to prove that each of our schools could make a difference!

After an initial induction session organized by Dr Louise Stoll into the philosophy, principles and current state of research on the topic of school effectiveness the strategic management group — consisting of the eight secondary headteachers and project manager — began to work on such practical issues as agreeing how the funding was to be divided between the eight schools and what criteria was to be used to approve individual proposals. Capital budget plans were the first to be produced during the summer term 1993 based on the School Development Plan and it was with considerable interest that we shared our ideas and discussed our own particular projects. It was clear that St Mark's, unlike other schools, could not decide to undertake building works. Capital plans would have to focus on the provision of furnishings, furniture and equipment, such as lap-top computers, which could be left behind and put to good use by others if the school were to move out of the borough. It was agreed that the learning environment, particularly in the lower school, could be enhanced by carpeting classrooms and that the upper school, with its bank of south facing windows, could be provided with suitable curtaining. Of all the changes wrought by SMAD these two may well have had the most profound effect on raising staff and student morale, modifying student behaviour and ultimately on raising achievement.

Other items agreed by the project manager, aimed at promoting the St Mark's key areas of encouraging independent learning and improving literacy, were filing cabinets and folders, Amstrad Notepads and Power Books, classroom libraries and display boards. All could be of immediate use and benefit to students and had the effect of making SMAD tangible and visible from the very start. This undoubtedly helped the initiative to take root in the school and to keep its tenets in the forefront of staff and student thinking.

At the same time as the strategic planning meetings were taking place, heads were offered the opportunity to visit a variety of schools around the country that were working on particular areas of school improvement. At St Mark's, the level of parental support and involvement in the school had recently become a matter of concern. Consequently I chose to spend a day in a working-class area of Kingston-upon-Hull, visiting a school which could boast of considerable success in encouraging parents to be effective partners in the education of their children. Of particular interest was the use of parents in the classroom and the support offered by the LEA to sustain the partnership initiative.

Another visit encompassed two schools in the London borough of Havering which were participants in the Improving the Quality of Education for All (IQEA) project. The focus of the day was on flexible, resource-based learning, but it was the scheme involving individual student–tutor interviews, introduced at one school to lay the foundation for the development and implementation of effective learning strategies, which most impressed. Although such a scheme did not find its way into the St Mark's SMAD Project Plans, it turned up later in a variant form in our Ofsted Action Plan. Much was gained from these forays into far flung parts of the country — two days in Shropshire, day trips to Gateshead, Birmingham and Wakefield — not least because of the 'business' that was transacted *en route* by the heads, coordinators and project manager and the solidarity of purpose that such journeys undoubtedly engendered.

In order to support the project an extensive inset programme was drawn up for heads and school coordinators. Inevitably heads often found it difficult to find the time to attend such sessions and not all were an unqualified success. Given an audience ranging from teachers of a few years' experience to heads of a dozen years standing it was not surprising that some facilitators had difficulty in pitching their contributions at an appropriate level. This resulted in an element of dissatisfaction among the heads although it was recognized that the school coordinators undoubtedly gained much from these seminars. I was not alone in finding the inset provided specifically for the heads far more stimulating than any other. We were all mindful of the importance of leadership in achieving school improvement and the light thrown on this topic, for example by Sue Purves, Human Resources Manager of Zeneca Pharmaceuticals, enabled us to view our management roles with quite different eyes.

The residential conference for senior management teams and school coordinators in October 1993 was not without its traumas for two of the heads involved. Faced with increasing difficulties in their schools, the pressure to bring about change *now* was almost too much to bear. Colleague heads found themselves playing as much a supportive role as fuelling the vision of school improvement. Little did we know that barely two months later neither head would be in the post. From that point on, the collegiality felt on embarking on our journey to school improvement, the spirit which had united us in our common quest, all but disappeared. In the following months we each pursued our own plans and goals with little reference to our neighbours.

The June 1994 residential conference was a quite different affair, aimed at reviewing the impact of SMAD on our individual schools and planning its final phase and future. Unhappily for St Mark's, it coincided with a post-Ofsted monitoring visit by HMI and I was able to spend only a few hours with colleagues and coordinators weighing our successes and failures. In retrospect it is ironic that, while we were congratulating ourselves on the efficacy of our literacy scheme, the staging of two impressive celebration days, the establishment of a group of 'critical friends' among the staff to promote improved classroom practice and the widespread dissemination of SMAD objectives throughout the school community, HMI was concluding that the school was 'in need of special measures'.

The final term of SMAD, as far as the heads were concerned, was largely spent on evaluation, preparing the final report and participating in the National Conference which took place in November 1994 at the London Institute of Education. At the latter event, each school 'set up stall' and heads, coordinators and students contributed to a presentation of what their school had set out to do and what it had achieved. All the heads must have felt considerable pride at recognizing the new horizons that had been opened up in their own schools, crucially affecting their perceptions of themselves as learning communities; the professional development that the majority of coordinators had undergone; and, finally, the improvements wrought in students' involvement in their own learning. It was a satisfying conclusion to eighteen months of challenge and self-examination. All that was left to do was to ensure that the SMAD principles and practices lived on.

Life after SMAD

From the start, St Mark's found itself in a more fortunate position than its neighbours in having two school-based SMAD coordinators rather than one, the rationale for this decision being the split site. The workload was thereby shared, mutual support guaranteed and the impact of the initiative doubled. By including one of the coordinators in the senior management team, project plans were routinely discussed at the highest level and progress reported on a regular basis. SMAD quickly became a standard item on every meeting agenda. This was in stark contrast to the situation which pertained in one or two other schools where access to the decision-making body was limited and where coordinators occasionally felt themselves to be waging a lone and losing battle.

When the project came to an end in December 1994 one of the coordinators left St Mark's for a new post. It was the unanimous decision of governors and senior staff that the remaining coordinator should retain her position on the senior management team and receive an enhanced salary to ensure that the initiative continued. By this time she had already established her credentials as an effective agent of change and as a consequence had been charged with the responsibility of implementing that part of the school's revised Action Plan concerned with pupil achievement.

The focus of the project has now been narrowed to three areas — the improvement of literacy in Years 7 and 8, extended day activities/revision centres, and the 'critical friends' scheme. The first two initiatives have proceeded apace. They were written into the St Mark's Action Plan and are now an accepted part of the school's overall provision for its students. The 'critical friends' scheme, although it too was included in the Action Plan, has proved difficult to sustain. The circumstances in which the school found itself in the months following the HMI monitoring visit in June 1994 caused a number of staff who had offered themselves as guinea pigs at the start of the scheme to resign from their posts and leave. Few colleagues now wish to subject themselves to further professional scrutiny, *albeit* voluntarily.

Dreams and Nightmares

The lifetime of the SMAD project coincided with a period of uncertainty and high drama at St Mark's. Although the pursuit of the dream of a single-site school occupied much time and energy, it did serve to buoy our efforts to bring about school improvement. Once the legislation was in place to permit the transfer of the school, spirits were raised and the serious business of planning the new St Mark's got underway. SMAD was able to capitalize on this feeling of optimism and excitement and project initiatives were eagerly seized on in the battle for self-improvement. In many ways, the project could not have come at a better time. A willing staff, already accommodated to a climate of change and inclined to greater collegiality as a result of a common purpose, ensured that the management of the initiative in its early stages was relatively straightforward.

Ofsted inspection came and went. The requisite Action Plan was drawn up and every member of the teaching staff was quite deliberately involved in the delivery of its targets, initially through designated working groups. We attempted to adopt SMAD recommended practices, to incorporate ideas culled from visits and inset, and to encourage the participation of all stakeholders in the formulation and implementation of new policies. We made steady, if occasionally slow, progress aiming to have new systems and structures in place for the start of the Autumn Term 1994. These would then have a term in which to embed themselves before we moved to our new and splendid surroundings.

The bombshell, when it came, was swift and wholly devastating. HMI, on a monitoring visit, just a month before the end of the Summer Term, deemed that insufficient progress had been made in remedying the weaknesses identified in the Ofsted report and placed the school under 'special measures'. Three weeks into the summer holiday the new Secretary of State, Gillian Shephard, rejected the transfer proposal. By the start of September, Hammersmith and Fulham had decided to propose to cease to maintain the school on the grounds of surplus places. All our brave ideals, all our hopes and aspirations had apparently brought St Mark's not to the verge of achieving the SMAD charter mark but to the very brink of closure.

Curiously, the blow dealt us by HMI served to concentrate minds and energies on the task in hand. There was a great sense of injustice, of there being 'another agenda' and consequently a great determination to prove our accusers wrong. This engendered the staff cohesiveness so critical to success.

The SMAD initiatives in the Autumn Term 1994, the final term of the project, were caught up in this surge of activity. The literacy scheme was more successful than ever before. Tasks incorporated in the revised Action Plan based on SMAD principles 'took off'. It could clearly be seen that SMAD driven and financed projects were contributing to progress and raised levels of achievement. In March 1995, staff efforts were vindicated. HMI returned and a publicly acknowledged the considerable results of our labours. Moreover, school improvement had been achieved against a background of threatened redundancy, in the context of a falling roll, and of a fast diminishing body of permanent staff.

Post Note

For a few brief weeks we dared to believe that St Mark's would be reprieved to plan and build on the foundations of SMAD reforms for another 150 years. But it was not to be. Three days before Easter 1995, the Secretary of State upheld the borough's proposal to cease to maintain the school on the grounds of surplus places.

This head's story is not the stuff of fairy tale. St Mark's will soon be no more. But the SMAD project will have imprinted itself on the collective memory of staff and students alike. It survived at St Mark's in spite of and, ironically, because of the trials which beset us and in retrospect can be seen to have contributed in no small way to genuine change.

The Coordinator's Story

Getting Going

For us, the story of Schools Make a Difference (SMAD) at St Mark's began on 26th March 1993, when I was appointed SMAD coordinator and Mike Dick was appointed assistant coordinator. Mike had been teaching at the school for fourteen years and was at the time the head of Year 11. I had been at the school just eighteen months and was the head of the English department.

We decided our first priority must be to raise awareness of the initiative as it was vitally important that all stakeholders were fully consulted and felt a sense of ownership of the project; Mike and I felt that we were stewards of the initiative but it belonged to all.

We had access to two budgets, one for capital expenditure and the other for revenue and knew that that areas identified for improvement had to be linked to our existing School Development Plan (SDP). (See Chapter 3 for more details of these budgets.) The priority areas we had identified in the SDP were to do with the management and monitoring of learning; assessment; and the raising of achievement and esteem through encouraging students to take responsibility for their own learning and behaviour.

We were also aware that because of our impending move to another site (as we believed at the time), discussed earlier in this chapter by Lesley Mortimer, there was no point in spending our capital budget on permanent building works or fixtures. I produced a brief, outlining the two focus areas with some suggestions to provoke discussion and invite comment. The initial ideas on which we worked came about from informal conversations with staff. I then made a presentation at a curriculum management meeting and heads of departments were asked to include SMAD on their next department meeting agendas to produce additional ideas.

Having made these approaches we felt it necessary to speak to all staff, and so, on 13th April 1993, I spoke at the upper school staff briefing and Mike spoke to the lower school staff. We were sensitive to the fact that not all colleagues will speak out in such situations. We also wished to include non-teaching staff who would not all be at the meeting. We consequently enlisted the expertise of the technology team and produced posters for both staffrooms on which everyone was invited to jot down ideas. We received many serious and workable ideas this way as well as one from a member of the support staff who suggested that in order to raise the 'spirits' of the staff there should be a cocktail bar installed in both common rooms . . .

We were keen that the students should be involved as much as possible in SMAD, and first introduced the project to the students in year assemblies. They were then encouraged to discuss their ideas during tutor and personal and social education periods and their suggestions were discussed at school council meetings.

We also tried to consult with governors and parents but were more successful with the first group. Mike was teacher–governor for the duration of the project and this ensured regular feedback and discussion at this forum. One of the other parent–governors took responsibility for liaising with parents although this was an area that never really took off.

We took down the posters in the staffrooms after a period of two weeks and discussed them with the headteacher. Certain ideas were deemed unfeasible or perhaps better supported by other initiatives. We had invited suggestions and did not want the stakeholders to feel that their ideas had not been considered but the brief was to begin new developments which were aligned to the School Development Plan (SDP).

Having prioritized these initial ideas we called a meeting of all interested people who attended in their own time on a Wednesday after school. More than half of the staff (including, we were pleased to note, all the heads of year who were intent on representing the views of their respective year groups) attended this and subsequent meetings.

At one of the early meetings with all the SMAD coordinators we had agreed to use a common Project Plan proforma. This was a document of some ten pages which was organized into sections requiring detail on how staff, pupils and parents had been consulted, costings, and how the bids addressed equal opportunities issues. Our first mistake at our after school meeting at St Mark's was to ask our colleagues to complete this original proforma. Our volunteers' goodwill was stretched to the limit but at the end of the session we were beginning to gain an idea of what our key areas would be.

By the end of the first meeting, different members of staff undertook to research costs and bring them to the next meeting. At our second meeting we had to eliminate bids by discussing educational as well as financial concerns. We were faced with the dilemma that we had to balance this process with ensuring that colleagues felt their efforts were valued. This was a useful process as it allowed for open and frank dialogue to take place, perhaps more succinctly put by Louis and Miles (1990):

> *shared* images of what the school should become are an important feature guiding successful improvement.

While this process was happening we regularly met with the coordinators from the other project schools and were constantly reassured and supported by each other. Through the inservice arranged for us we became more aware of the research on school effectiveness and school improvement and became increasingly able to draw on it to inform our practice.

During the summer term, ideas for our Project Plan began to take shape and we finally submitted the capital plan in July and the revenue in October 93. It all took much longer than expected but we took heart from the research which indicated that the process was almost as important as the product! We focused on areas directly affecting the students, improving the learning environment and directly affecting the staff.

Throughout the project we were affected by other agendas (all previously discussed by the head, Lesley Mortimer). Firstly, a proposal to move from our split site to a single site in another borough; then the announcement of an impending Ofsted inspection which we 'passed'. This was followed by a HMI follow-up visit when the bombshell that we were deemed 'requiring special measures' was announced. Shortly after this visit, the Secretary of State pronounced that she would not give permission for us to move and the local authority, faced with a serious surplus place issue, then announced proposals for our closure. Although at the time of writing (April 1995) we have had an encouraging feedback from the most recent HMI visit we have just been informed that the school will be closed in August 1995. All these events have undoubtedly had an impact on staff morale and affected what we were able to do as part of a school improvement project. Nevertheless we tried, and what follows is an open and honest account of our efforts.

What We Did

Strategies directly affecting students

From the consultation process we decided to address five areas: improving literacy skills; enhancing information technology (IT) capability; raising self-esteem through celebration events; providing facilities for after school and holiday study; and involving the students in improving the learning environment.

1 Improving Literacy

Our first aim was to improve literacy. Infant age children who are finding it hard to conquer the skills of reading and writing are not so far behind their classmates because they are all beginners but by the time the students get to secondary school this gap is exacerbated. This creates a feeling of failure which has a profound effect on self-esteem and learning throughout the curriculum. As Marie Clay (1986) writes in her book, a diagnostic survey of children experiencing difficulty in beginning reading should be undertaken when the children have been in school for one year otherwise 'unbalanced ways of operating on print can become habituated if practised day after day. They are resistant to change and this can happen in the first twelve to eighteen months of instruction.'

This then was our situation; according to assessment on entry, more than half of our intake was presenting reading difficulties. Their 'unbalanced way of operating on print' had been set. (While the secondary schools in the borough were participating in SMAD, the primary schools were involved in a Reading Recovery project and consequently we hope that the problems we were encountering at the time of writing will soon be a thing of the past.)

Class libraries   On our visits to 'interesting' schools around the country, we came across some which had instituted whole school reading where *all* members of staff as well as students stopped what they were doing and read for a prescribed time. We wanted to introduce this idea but thought it judicious to start with the lower school. We consequently decided to provide all Year 7 and 8 tutor groups with class libraries. The school librarian took responsibility for finding books which represented the diverse cultures of our students.

We soon realized that this initiative would have been even more successful if we had involved a representative number of students to help choose the books because they are the audience and would have a much clearer idea of what they and their peers would consider to be exciting reading material. We therefore invited the students to make suggestions for purchases for their own tutor groups and we were able to provide accordingly. It also emerged that plays would have been a useful addition to these libraries to encourage shared reading. We consequently purchased sets for each tutor group which have proved to be an extremely valuable resource, encouraging collaboration and shared learning between students of differing abilities within the same tutor group.

Once our class libraries were ready, the second in charge of the English department ran an induction programme for tutors. In order to raise the status of the scheme in the eyes of the students, 'Captain Book' (otherwise known as the second–in–charge of the English department) dressed in somewhat startling garb, visited assemblies and the PSE lessons when the class libraries were being used. His visits were undoubtedly memorable and helped to remind the students that reading can be fun.

To link this initiative with a move to enhance literacy across the curriculum we supplied dictionaries and encyclopaedias to every teaching base as we felt that these texts would be of use in all curriculum areas. We were gratified by the response received from colleagues —

for example, the science teaching programme now includes a focus on scientific vocabulary and spelling.

Paired reading   We originally targeted Years 7 and 8 students but then Mike (head of Year 11) realized it would be a good idea to involve volunteer Year 11 students in partnership reading with the lower school students. The concept was not just to support the students with literacy problems but to enrich the reading of the able pupils too. In fact, one Year 7 pupil explained the meaning of a word to a Year 11 student!

The second-in-charge of the English department ran inset for the Year 11 students, on mentoring and coaching skills. They then met their partners during the weekly PSE period. All students reported how much they enjoyed the experience (and not just the ones hoping to start a career in caring). In fact they only stopped participating in the scheme when the pressures of exam coursework deadlines became too great. The following year we invited both Year 10 and 11 students to join the scheme which ensured greater continuity when the exam season started.

What the students thought   Although the scheme was generally well received — Alicia in Year 8 said that 'children were not interested in reading so this is a good idea' — it was not without its critics. Charles in the same tutor group felt that some of the texts were 'boring' and suggested that we invest in some 'smaller' books. Some students suggested additions to the libraries, for example horror books, and others thought a democratic process of book buying should be introduced. According to Russell, 'A list should be brought around so people can write what kind of books they like.' This idea has since been responded to.

The success of this scheme really depended on the effectiveness of the tutor and we realized the importance of the teacher's key role in presenting it with enthusiasm. We also realized that we should have been monitoring the programme much more closely and perhaps taken a bit more heed of Michael Fullan's advice about applying the right balance of pressure and support with our colleagues. Nevertheless we were pleased with what we had achieved.

This scheme has had a dramatic effect upon the English department's lessons. Many of the English periods now begin with silent reading time using the class libraries supplied by SMAD. One teacher, for example, has developed this initiative by compiling her own class libraries from English department stock that have been selected to encourage and challenge her students. She starts every lesson with a short period of silent or paired/group reading which sets a particular ethos for the rest of the lesson.

The tutor group/class book initiative implemented during SMAD was deemed to be so successful by students and staff alike because of the way that it has encouraged reading, not just in English lessons, and had an impact on students' attitudes to work. We therefore decided to carry on with it after the formal part of the project had finished.

2 Enhancing information technology capability for students with special needs

Our second strategy was to enhance the information technology (IT) capability of our students. Because of the proposed move to another site it was not considered practical to spend money on establishing a technology suite. We decided, therefore, that purchasing portable machines would be more appropriate. Our plan was twofold; firstly, to work with seven students all of whom had statements of special needs and allow them to carry the machines from lesson to lessons; secondly, to enhance IT provision in targeted areas of the curriculum.

The seven 'Power books' for the statemented students arrived in November and we then planned a training session for pupils, staff and the parents of the 'Power book' users. This was successful for those people who were able to attend including one parent. The scheme started particularly well for the pupil whose parent benefited from some training. At the beginning, the scheme was less popular with the other students who did not immediately realize how the machines could help them. Our original concerns that they might feel stigmatized at being singled out for special treatment were not manifested and, as the pro-file of the machines in the school increased, the desirability to 'own' one of these expensive machines became overwhelming for some. One of the statemented students who was gaining most from this IT facility had his machine stolen from him on school premises. This made us rethink the scheme. Instead of being carried at all times by individual pupils, the machines are now held by me and students come and ask to use them in particular lessons. Being more familiar with the machines and what they can do has given them more confidence and they are in continual demand. Trevor, in Year 10, pronounced his verdict: 'Its really helped my work a lot. I think it's brilliant.'

According to some colleagues, the other IT thrust of SMAD, having access to portable IT equipment in the classroom, was extremely suc-cessful. This comment from a member of the humanities department was not untypical.

I used my Amstrad Notepads first in my Year 9 geography lessons with the special needs students only. The change was remarkable, from little or no work these students were now producing much more and then sticking it in their books. Later in the academic year I extended the use of the machines to any student who asked in Year 9 and so had to devise a rotating system with a measure of success. The students willingness to use a keyboard certainly seems to be a strong motivating factor in output of written work. I feel that in ideal circumstances the 'Notepads' are a constructive tool for motivating not only the less able students but indeed all students.

We increased staff training on these machines by operating drop-in sessions in the IT room and more informal encouragement and support in the staffroom. Now a number of departments have integrated IT resources into their lessons. As this good practice is disseminated, more students and staff are keen to have access to the machines.

3 Celebration days

We recognized that as a staff we had to address the issue of our expectations of students but also agreed with Michael Barber (1993), that on its own this was not enough. If a student has low self-esteem but is faced with high expectations from their teacher, she or he will become demoralized very quickly. High expectations must be matched by high self-esteem. We appreciated that raising self-esteem was not in itself going to raise student achievement but hoped it would be seen as an impetus for curriculum and relationship development. We hoped to motivate students by confirming the strengths of their cultural and social background.

Having discussed these issues, the working party decided to mount two celebration days that would target and celebrate the achievement of groups of people in our society who are often stereotyped and portrayed as losers or failures in the traditional areas of our lives.

> Far too much discouragement is evident in the classroom because teachers feel their pupils lack role models in their home and communities. (Kuykendall, 1991)

We were concerned that our students did not have frequent access to successful role models from similar backgrounds. We wanted to emphasize that high achievement is not beyond them. We perceived the days as a role model exercise with the message, 'If we can achieve so can you!' We devised a plan to explode the myth that inner-city pupils are going to fail.

Celebrating Black achievement   For our first celebration day we decided to focus on 'Black Achievement'. Mike had been enthused by a visit to The Hammersmith School's 'Celebration Evening' and we decided to build on their experience. (This is just one example of the successful 'networking' relationships that developed between the coordinators; we were all keen to share our ideas and appreciate the progress of each others' school. This interest has been maintained despite the official ending of the project.)

Once this idea was agreed, Mike and I called upon the help of volunteer staff to set up a whole school celebration day. There was considerable response and the SMAD working party met every Wednesday lunchtime to organize the event. Responsibilities were shared and we decided to organize different events on the two school sites, giving the upper school students more career orientated workshops and the lower school more recreational ones. The working party did not wish to perpetuate the stereotype of the Black achiever just being good at sport and music and so successful role models were invited from industry, education, commerce, sport, and the entertainment field. The workshops included 'hair, health and beauty', cookery, circus clowns, soccer coaching, magicians, law, commerce, and drama, with our main guest celebrity being Chris Eubank with his own inimitable style. It was made clear right from the outset that this was not just a day for 'Black Achievers' but must be seen as a day that would act as an impetus for all to achieve.

The day was a success, both on the part of students and guests. In their evaluation many students were extremely positive and asked for more celebration days. Although we found the organization of a whole school event on a split-site very difficult and time-consuming, we certainly felt it was worthwhile. The evaluation sheets distributed to both students and staff, from which we obtained almost 100 per cent response rate, were very positive. Diana in Year 10 wrote what she enjoyed most of all, 'Was seeing what these people achieved in life'. Kofi in the same year agreed saying that he enjoyed, 'Seeing what these people had achieved and next year I'm going to be there'.

The strengths of the day as perceived by staff were the:

- Number and variety of Black people in school
- Interaction between achievers and pupils and the range of experiences available

- The enthusiasm of the pupils and the staff organizing the event
- That pupils got a lot out of the day.

The working party decided that the feedback was positive enough for us to consider mounting another celebration day learning from the lessons of this one. In particular we would need to be more structured and encourage the students to be involved in more activities and workshops. Staff were keen offer their support, largely in terms of their subject specialism. Because of this, and comments such as 'We should have something like this even more often', we were determined to get the second day right.

Celebrating women's achievement Our second celebration focused upon 'Women's Achievement'. This area of achievement was particularly important for us as we suffer from a significant gender imbalance; the boys outnumber the girls by three to two. This time the emphasis was was less upon celebrities and more on skills and the contributions made by women in the past, present and future. Contacts given by the careers office were followed up; women in manual trades were invited in; Mike had contact with England's womens' rugby coach; the music teacher invited in a female dance teacher; an ex-pupil of the school ran a gospel singing workshop and sang in the morning assembly which was led by a female priest; the science department volunteered to run a workshop on women in science; the art department ran one on women in art; and the male staff in the technology department ran a cookery workshop. A company called Artsbrush were also in attendance developing drama, music and art skills. Almost everyone in the school community was involved, including a supply teacher who volunteered to collect something needed for the day. We saw this as an indication of the importance people placed on this day; their commitment to the principles behind the day and their willingness to be involved.

We learned a lot from our first attempt at organizing whole school events and the second day was a much more tightly organized affair. The day opened with women leading the assembly and worship, and the day ended with students sharing what they had learned. This was particularly effective with the history group who played a game called, 'Who is She?' Several of the boys addressed the whole school assembly beginning with the sentence, 'I learned today that . . .', and completed the sentence with a variety of statements such as, 'I didn't realize women had done so much'.

Staff considered the strengths of the day were:

A relaxed atmosphere and good organization/timing.

A wide range of activities and a distinct difference between morning and afternoon activities.

The dancing teacher and students were excellent, the students enjoyed it. The afternoon session really worked well.

We wanted to raise the profile of SMAD and at the same time heighten awareness of the potential of our students. We found that organizing such an event not only achieved this but also acted as a catalyst and encouraged collegiality and collaboration amongst the whole school community. Having had such a sharp focus and having raised awareness of how two specific groups had achieved success, we are now sustaining the idea of celebrating the success of all of our students. In assemblies we are consciously mentioning all aspects of achievement whether it be academic, sporting or social (this applies to students *and* staff). All staff/departments have been encouraged to display good work and this has improved the environment and enabled the students to take greater pride in their school. (See the evaluator's discussion of these celebratory events in Chapter 6.)

4 Extended day provision
In the Study Support pack written for the Prince's Trust by Professor John MacBeath (1993) he suggests ten success criteria for school-based study centres.

1 To give students a place to study.
2 To give students access to resources.
3 To provide opportunities for students to study and learn together.
4 To provide students with tutor/teacher support.
5 To tackle a problem of student underachievement.
6 To offer quality time to a specific group.
7 To enhance learning and teaching through improved study skills.
8 To improve student–teacher relationships.
9 To improve examination performance.
10 To help students develop greater self-confidence.

We found this list useful and it helped focus our planning. We decided to use part of the allocated budget for extended day and revision centres to appoint a tutor in charge. We did this by open advertisements for all staff; one for the extended day provision and one for the revision centre. Appointments were made quickly and the tutors-in-charge immediately addressed the task in hand by organizing and publicizing the provision. We were able to pay teachers from the SMAD budget a modest sum for coming in during the holidays and an even more modest sum for running after school activities.

St Mark's held its first revision centre in the first four days of the Easter holiday in 1993. The core subjects were all represented as were religious education, music, geography and history. The following year our second revision centre, also held for four days, was supported by more subjects and more pupils. We were delighted with the huge numbers of students who turned up. The students arrived with a very positive attitude and worked dilegently throughout the sessions. We experienced no behaviour problems at all.

I found that the atmosphere was nice with helpful teachers. When you're at home alone, you can't get help. (Scot)

It was very good and helpful. I needed to catch up. At home I would have said 'the next day, and the next day'. (Ahmed)

(Nalini seemed to sum it up) I would definitely recommend it.

Ever since the teacher's action, our after school provision has been very fragmented. However with the appointment of a tutor-in-charge, many departments started running after school clubs again. These were mostly for upper school pupils with some new developments such as homework and technology clubs. Lower school activities were provided mainly at lunchtimes.

The extended day programme at St Mark's has proved to be very successful. This was borne out by the Keele survey (a survey administered by Keele University to ascertain pupil perceptions of school life). 71 per cent of students at St Mark's said that they were provided with opportunities to undertake extra-curricular activities. This compared favourably with the University's national data base which showed 56 per cent of students answering the same way.

Twelve teachers and two support staff were involved in organizing and conducting the activities which attracted between 70 and 100 pupils per week. The activities offered were: art, computing, mathematics, music, science, soccer, technology and a general homework club. We evaluated this provision by asking all pupils who attended to complete a questionnaire. The following are a selection of pupils' responses:

Why did you attend?

- To finish off work, to get individual help, to understand work.
- To do extra work on coursework.
- Because I needed to catch up with my work, and to have particular work explained.
- To complete coursework.
- To do more art for my exam work
- To play on some instruments and to practise.
- Because I enjoy it and it is helpful.

What have you enjoyed about the club(s) you attended?

- I get to finish what I started.
- Extra time to work.
- They were interesting, understandable and peaceful.
- They offer more time to experiment with different ideas.
- Being able to listen music when I work.
- The individual help.
- More time is spent on individuals so they can understand things better.
- Doing extra work at my own pace.
- You can do what you want within the subject.

Do you think extended day clubs and activities are important or worthwhile?

- Yes, because you get a lot more done than if you were at home.
- They are important as they help you a lot with class work.
- They are important because you can do what you did not do in the classroom.

How would you feel if extended day clubs and activities were stopped? and why?

- Terrible. I would have to rely on myself. There are a lot of distractions outside of school and my work would not be of a very high standard.

- I would be disappointed because they offer alternatives to expand what you do.
- It should not be stopped because it is the only chance to finish your work.

Would you attend the extended day clubs and activities if they were held again next academic year?
Every single response was: 'YES!'

What type of clubs and activities would you like to see being held in the future?
Most responses asked for 'more of the same' but a few asked for enrichment classes in non-exam subjects such as cookery, drama and dance.

Undoubtedly the after school provision has been successful and staff have agreed to carry on even when the extra funding finishes. The notion of an extended day has become part of our Action Plan in response to Ofsted. Following Ofsted, one of our key issues is that the school 'should adopt and implement strategies to raise pupils' standard of achievement . . .' — one strategy we have already put in place is a homework club for the lower school. We intend somehow to continue funding Easter revision centres catering specifically for Year 11 students.

Improving the learning environment
The lower school is a Victorian three-tiered building in a somewhat sorry state of repair. At the time of SMAD, as already discussed, we were anticipating moving to another site. Any changes to the physical environment, therefore, had to be removable. However, during the consultation period it emerged that there was a widespread feeling that carpets and curtains would have an immediate and dramatic effect on improving the learning environment. Tubs of plants, seating and student lockers were also requested. Our intention was that we would all return to a physically enhanced environment in September, therefore our priority was to make the physical improvements happen over the summer holiday. We had canvassed students beforehand regarding colour coordination, and petrol-blue and indigo were favourite.

However, all was not plain sailing. Due to our inexperience we did not proof-read our capital bid. We omitted to check figures and discovered that the figures submitted for the refurbishment of the school for carpets *and* curtains was in fact for only *one* room! This was not the only miscalculation made. Although it was wonderful to have access to a generous budget to improve our environment, spending the money proved more complicated and certainly time-consuming than envisaged. Despite both of us being heads of department and having experience of capitation, we really needed administrative help to manage the budget. These obstacles set back the installations as a summer holiday date became impossible. After one false start, when the fitters arrived without the carpet (!), they were eventually installed over two weekends in October 1993. The picnic benches and lockers had to be sacrificed for a number of reasons; most importantly, because of the expenditure required for the carpet and curtains. Fullan was right; change is messy!

The response to this aspect of the project was entirely favourable. Mike interviewed the cleaners and the site care manager to discover their response. The site care manager, admitted that he had had initial misgivings but was pleasantly surprised how well the students took care of their environment and believed that the general tidiness of the building had improved. Likewise, the cleaners were also pleased, although the 'chewing gum problem' had not disappeared. Students were delighted with the impact. Clare Sanders, a Year 9 student, said, 'When the room looks nice, and the floor is clean, you feel like working, you feel like putting your bag down on the floor without worrying about the dirt.' Paul Douglas, in Year 10, said, 'Curtains Make a Difference!'

The carpets and curtains continue to give great value for money; both enhancing the student and staff comfort and providing the students with a form-base of which to be proud. We have encouraged all parties to continue to look after the area around their teaching or form base. We hope that, for the students, having the facilities to display their work in a attractive environment will encourage increased self-esteem and pride in their work.

This has been a difficult part of the project to evaluate objectively but we feel that student levels of morale have been raised and a tour around the buildings reveal attractive classrooms with students' work displayed. The physical improvements were undoubtedly beneficial but of crucial importance was the involvement of the students in the decision-making process.

Strategies directly affecting staff

There were two key areas of staff development in the project plan: the 'critical friend' scheme and staff inset to support the aims of the project. We were eager to develop a 'critical friend' scheme for staff as improving teaching and learning were strong features of our School Development Plan. In September 1993 the SMAD coordinators and their headteachers attended an inset led by David Hopkins from the Institute of Education at Cambridge on 'School Improvement' and part of his presentation featured the 'critical friend' scheme for staff. In its simplest term it is an arrangement that allows colleagues to observe each others' lessons, but in a way which is likely to be less formal and hopefully less threatening than other types of classroom observation.

We were keen to initiate this scheme because we believed it was an important step along the journey to school improvement as described by Bruce Joyce (1991). We felt that it would assist in the evolution of a 'collaborative culture' which would promote a climate that fostered achievement and excellence for both staff and students. Supportive relationships are clearly an important feature in the culture of an effective school, which is what we were endeavouring to create. Judith Warren Little (1982) believes that school improvement is more easily effected when teachers 'plan, design, research, evaluate . . . prepare materials together' and 'frequently observe each other and provide each other with useful (if potentially frightening) evaluations of their teaching'.

We decided to start observing each other. In this case, 'we' meant volunteer members of the SMAD working party. By this time we had just about survived a bruising Ofsted experience and it was essential that observations were seen to be mutual and supportive. There were nine of us in the group representing a variety of subject areas: English, mathematics, physical education, science, music, religious education and geography. A broad range of the teaching hierarchy — including middle managers, a standard national scale teacher and a member of the senior management team — were represented in the group. Decisions had to be made as to who would partner who. Teachers of practical subjects and teachers of similar or the same subjects chose each other for partners and where possible decided to observe a class that they themselves taught being taught by their partner. Because of the uneven number of the group, one partnership was actually a 'threesome'.

We met with Kate Myers, the project manager and agreed the following ground rules.

- Absolute confidentiality — observer or observed not to discuss with anyone else what happened in lesson, without explicit permission of partner.
- Focus of oservation to be negotiated. As partnership becomes established so should trust, and flexibility to mention issues that arise outside focus.

- Proformas for recording to be agreed by partners.
- Reliability — once arrangements are made, partners must stick to them. Be there and stay there!
- Lesson plans if available to be shared.
- Written evidence to be given to the observed, no copies made. Observed responsible for retrieval for follow-up sessions.

We then had to organize supply cover and coordinate a timetable. This was not a process that was easy to manage; the split site again caused problems. In order to make maximum use of the supply teacher, the classes to be observed had to be based at either the lower or upper school for the whole morning or afternoon. There was also a tension when on one of the days on which we had planned to observe, many teachers were absent. It was suggested that observations should be cancelled to ensure the smooth running of the school. I was resistant to the idea, not simply because of all the complex planning that had been involved in organizing the day, but also because it implied something about how the scheme was perceived: if it seemed to some that it could so easily be rescheduled, then perhaps the importance of it had been undervalued. I was able to reorganize the cover!

The observations did take place, largely as scheduled, and there was informal feedback from the participants. Two months later, when we had all completed at least one observation, we enjoyed a more detailed and formal evaluation of our experiences. Kate Myers chaired a meeting of the 'critical friends' and the brief was to report on progress so far.

Some teachers said they had hoped to pick up effective strategies sometimes for dealing with groups they found difficult. We heard comments, such as, 'I think it's amazing how you started that group off. I'm going to try that.' Others were hoping to validate their own experience: 'They're as horrible with you as they are with me', which moved on to a discussion about what are *we* going to do about it. Each observation differed greatly: one teacher found himself participating in the lesson rather than watching it; in fact he played the drums! The recording of observations also varied. Some colleagues detailed the minutiae of the lesson, whilst others simply jotted down notes. Some partners had had the opportunity to give and receive feedback, but the majority felt that they would like a longer period of time to engage in talk and discussion with their partners. We found that colleagues wanted to be 'frequently engaged in talk about teaching' (Jakicic, 1994). Teachers can enjoy a sense of achievement by recognizing publicly and documenting the accomplishments of their colleagues. We also found that being engaged in a common purpose with colleagues one did not normally work with, and because of our split site, hardly knew, allowed opportunities for supportive interaction to teachers who had previously felt isolated.

The 'critical friend' scheme has now been incorporated into our post-Ofsted Action Plan concerned with the improvement of the quality of teaching.

Staff Inservice

School based　Our Project Plan, linked with our School Development Plan had a focus on promoting positive behaviour and raising self-esteem. We had started to address this through the celebration days discussed earlier and subsequently wanted to consolidate upon the progress we had made. We decided to work on this during our professional training day in May 1994.

Through word-of-mouth recommendation we found a consultant, Jenny Mosely, who facilitated a highly effective and productive day for us. We explored the issue about what made for a good relationship between a student and teacher and we decided it is based on support and action. We followed this with the question 'What can staff offer each other?' Among other things, we decided on personal development and honesty. The second half of the session was spent on how to raise self-esteem. We drew up a draft code of conduct which has provided the basis for continued dialogue, and decisions that were made on the day have been absorbed into the school's behaviour policy. At the end of the session Jenny received a spontaneous round of applause — not an anticipated response from a potentially disillusioned and demoralized staff. An idea which came from this day, 'Circle Time', has already been used by Years 8 and 9 in their PSE lessons.

The Haggerston School conference　Haggerston School in East London organizes an annual conference on one Saturday in October, related to school improvement. We decided to use the project funds to sponsor any staff who wanted to attend and were very gratified that fourteen staff elected to give up a Saturday to do so. The first conference, 'Improving from Within', that we attended had Roland Barth from Harvard University as the keynote speaker. Staff were really enthused and motivated by this day and the following year a similar number attended the next conference hosted by Peter Mortimore and Michael Barber. This time we found we had something to cont ribute and were not just listening to the experts. Somehow I found myself 'volunteered' to talk about our 'critical friends' initiative in front of a packed hall!

Visits to 'interesting' schools   Visits to schools that were addressing issues similar to us were arranged for all the coordinators. With a member of our project working party we visited two such schools in Birmingham. This was particularly valuable as we were able to see examples of good ideas in practice and at least one idea, 'teachers adopting borderline students' (TABS), was brought back to our school for implementation. This scheme was put into practice with Year 11. Students who were likely to gain C or D grades in their impending examinations were identified and 'adopted' by volunteer teachers. The pairs met at least weekly where progress and problems were discussed. This scheme has been continued with the current Year 11.

Keeping it going

From the beginning we realized that the project was a pump-priming one and that the school needed to keep the SMAD initiative alive when the funding ceased. Indeed there had to be 'Life after SMAD'. The importance the school placed in this project is recognized by the integral role many of the key issues have in the School Action Plan, for example the 'critical friends' scheme, TABs, and the literacy initiative.

In conclusion, as coordinators we have learned that we can be effective change agents. SMAD enabled us to articulate and attempt to put into practice a vision, shared by us all.

References

Barber, M. (1993) 'Great expectations', *Education*, 30th July.

Clay, M. (1986) *The Early Detection of Reading Difficulties*, London, Heinneman.

Kuykendall, C. (1991) *Improving Black Student Achievement*, Washington DC, The Mid-Atlantic Equity Center.

Jakicic, C. (1994) 'Taking small steps to promote collaboration', *Journal of Staff Development*, Vol 15.

Joyce, B. (1991) 'The doors to school improvement', *Educational Leadership*, Vol 48, No. 8.

Little, J.W. (1982) 'Norms of collegiality and experimentation: workplace conditions of school success', *American Educational Research Journal*, Vol 19 No. 3, pp. 325–40.

MacBeath, J. (1993) *Inspiring Young People: A Place for Success. An Evaluation of Study Support in England, Scotland and Northern Ireland*, London, The Prince's Trust.

Louis, K. and Miles, M.B. (1992) *Improving The Urban High School: What Works and Why*, London, Cassell.

6   The Evaluator's View

Keith Pocklington

Introduction

The Remit for the Evaluation

The external evaluation was commissioned at the outset of the project by the project manager, on behalf of the LEA. The main requirement was for a formative evaluation to be conducted by an independent source, employing a mainly qualitative approach to data collection — notably, semi-structured interviews of the key staff and a sample of students — with a view to informing the development and evolution of the scheme itself. This was to be achieved by means of an interim written report and verbal reports to the project manager and school coordinators. Educational practices and the processes involved would be examined, partly with a view to developing an understanding of what was and was not happening and identifying the reasons why. In addition, at the end of the project a summative report would be prepared, in which would be recorded the main achievements of the initiative. (Further details about the methodology employed can be found in the Appendix, see pp. 156–7.)

The Nature of the Project

The *Schools Make a Difference* project (SMAD) was a scheme whose avowed intent was to lay the foundations for raising student levels of attainment, achievement and morale in all eight secondary schools in the London borough of Hammersmith and Fulham. It is against these objectives that the evaluation proceeded, though remaining alert to the possibility of unintended outcomes.

Outline of the Chapter

In the account that follows, having carefully weighed the evidence available, I begin by recording what appear to me to have been the main achievements of the project to date. I then go on to examine and report on the various factors that in my estimation are responsible for the success that has been achieved, or which have hindered progress being made. Four factors would appear to have been particularly influential, and accordingly are examined in some detail.

The central section of the chapter focuses upon the main developments that occurred in the schools, and is intended partly to illustrate something of the variation in respect of how the project played out in practice. The section commences on the modifications made to the physical environment of the schools, and considers the responses of students and staff to these. Next, the main initiatives that were targeted specifically on the students are reviewed, along with a judgment as to what each achieved. After having identified three areas in which intended developments were slow to come about, I raise a series of key questions and issues for consideration by all who are interested and/or involved in attempts at school improvement, whatever their nature and scale.

In the concluding section, I look to life beyond SMAD, and draw attention to various aspects of practice and a number of considerations which seem to me to be critical if the progress made under SMAD is to be sustained and built on.

What have been the Main Achievements to date of the SMAD Initiative?

It can be stated with confidence that differing rates of progress have been achieved across the eight schools. Some of the reasons for this variation are to be found in the next section, 'What factors appear to have aided or hindered the successful implementation of SMAD?'

General Benefits for Pupils

- There was an overall rise in student achievement across all of the borough's secondary schools in 1993/4. Although encouraging, care should, however, be exercised in ascribing this improvement to one or more aspects of the project. Whilst

SMAD components may well have contributed to the raising of achievement — for instance, there was some evidence to link attendance at revision centres with increased GCSE performance overall (in that the scores of students who attended such classes generally were noticeably higher than the scores of those students who did not attend) — nevertheless, in all probability, SMAD will be one of several relevant considerations. In any case it is feasible only to talk cautiously in terms of likely associations, and not cause and effect.

- The popularity amongst the students of revision centres and coursework clinics — mirrored, to a lesser extent, in relation to the extended day classes.
- The success of various forms of celebratory event held in some of the schools, particularly in relation to the less academically inclined and the poorly behaved among the students.
- The generally positive response amongst students to improvements to the physical environment of the schools.
- The emphasis placed in most of the schools on pupil consultation, including the development of student councils.
- Some evidence to suggest the beginnings of transforming the dominant ethos in the pupil sub-culture. Staff and students alike made mention of pupil motivation, commitment and self-esteem having been enhanced, of increased maturity and more responsible behaviour, together with greater enjoyment of school.

General Benefits for Teachers

- An acceptance that schools can — and do! — make a difference in terms of pupils' life chances, and that pupil achievement across the board can be raised. Further, a preparedness to consider seriously the question, 'What more can we do?', marks a notable shift in teacher thinking regarding underachievement amongst substantial numbers of pupils in the borough's secondary schools.
- SMAD has triggered debate upon topics and issues related to the purposes and functions of schools and schooling.
- SMAD has concentrated practitioners' thinking upon the related issues of teaching and learning and pupil achievement, stimulating some of them to take a hard look at the quality of the education being provided for students in their school. It

has led some teachers to experiment with approaches to teaching and learning, and to the production of curriculum materials and learning resources that are designed to increase student involvement in the learning process.

- Attention has also been devoted to issues to do with making school management more effective, including improved (i.e., strategic) planning and systematic follow-through (i.e., monitoring and evaluation). There is also some evidence of a shift toward more collegial approaches to school governance.
- For those teachers who have acted to coordinate SMAD within their school, it has proved to be empowering, and an invaluable piece of professional development.
- The creation of an effective, mutual cross-school support group among the SMAD coordinators.
- For other teachers who have had a direct involvement in SMAD-related activities and developments, there is evidence that for many it has refreshed and revitalized, raised morale and left them also feeling empowered.
- There is some evidence to suggest a shift in attitude, especially among senior managers, away from a preoccupation with problems, and toward the positive and developmental.
- The degree of active cooperation and sharing that has been forged across the eight schools.

What Factors Appear to have Aided or Hindered the Successful Implementation of SMAD?

Factors Aiding Development

Four factors stand out as having had a significant bearing upon the extent to which the project has met with success in the various schools. They are:

- the project having its own manager;
- the appointment of a SMAD coordinator in each school;
- the interplay between coordinator and headteacher;
- the establishment of a working party in each school to assist with the implementation of the project.

More generally, the conditions and circumstances which pertained in the individual school also exerted an influence over what transpired — as will become apparent.

The Project Manager

The project had its own, virtually full-time (80 per cent) manager. The person concerned, although a newcomer to the local authority, had prior experience of developing and coordinating national projects. It is significant that the role of project manager, as originally envisaged by the then chief inspector, went beyond simply exercising managerial responsibility. It was conceived of as being a catalyst — an 'animateur', someone who 'will make something happen', in the words of a senior officer.

The manner in which the person appointed duly fulfilled the role was very much in line with this conception of the chief inspector. She had the enthusiasm, determination and drive, also the expertise, to 'make things happen'. Crucially, she was able to strike a balance between giving a lead and encouraging and assisting others — notably, the coordinators in the schools — to exercise autonomy and initiative. Throughout, she invested time and care in negotiating a way forward that was acceptable to all concerned, and sought to be receptive to ideas or requests put forward by coordinators and headteachers and to respond positively, though all the while ensuring that the initiative as a whole retained its coherence in accordance with the basic tenets of the project.

Amongst this person's initial priorities were fostering a sense of shared ownership of the project among the eight headteachers, together with fashioning a team and building a working rapport out of what were, in many respects, eight very different individuals with contrasting personalities. Once the school coordinators had been appointed, the same approach was extended to them. In addition, originally the initiative had been sold to the heads by the chief inspector partly as management development for senior staff. This provision of training was another of the project manager's priorities, although in the event it was translated into exposing both heads and coordinators to the ideas and thinking behind the school effectiveness and school improvement literatures. The third priority initially was to assist each coordinator and headteacher to prepare the Project Plan for their school.

Once developments in the schools were up and running, it was a matter of maintaining an oversight of these, including keeping in view the broader picture, and sustaining the momentum. Attention to the latter was required to a greater or lesser extent depending on the capability of the individual coordinator, the degree of support forthcoming from the headteacher and/or senior colleagues, and the range and magnitude of the pressures affecting the school in question.

In all, several distinct strands concerning the role which the project manager fulfilled may be discerned. They include (in no particular order):

- Providing strategic management and oversight of the project.
- Providing vision and leadership — though with the aim of empowering other people.
- Putting forward ideas and suggestions that teachers were free to adopt and adapt or to ignore.
- Providing guidance and advice.
- Feeding in the broader perspective regarding developments nationally and internationally — in effect, raising sights beyond practice within the borough. In this she drew upon her extensive range of contacts and her sound knowledge of the research-based literature.
- Motivating and encouraging.
- Promoting cross-fertilization — in particular, across the eight schools, but also with schools beyond the borough.
- Balancing pressure and support; in particular, constantly urging all concerned to extend the boundaries beyond which people were prepared to settle.
- Acting as a sounding board.
- Providing linkage e.g., between practitioners and schools, both within and beyond the borough.
- Administering the scheme in its entirety (including bringing it to a close on time).
- Publicizing the venture, both within and beyond the borough.

Undoubtedly, having someone to lead the project, as well as oversee and manage it, has been crucial with respect to what has been accomplished thus far. Put simply, things would not have happened at the same rate or to the same extent had the project not had its own manager. This is no reflection on the coordinators or the headteachers; rather, of their different set of priorities.

However, although having a project manager has proved fully justified, and well as the postholder acquitted herself in discharging the role of animateur, there would appear to have been a downside. A number of reservations were expressed by teachers. One of the most common complaints of the school coordinators concerned the extent of the demands made on them. There were times when it had seemed as if the scale and scope of the project, together with the attendant demands, were threatening to get out of hand. While they recognized that the project manager was anxious to maximize the development of

SMAD, and hence its achievements, during the formal life-span of the project, nevertheless they felt at times that perhaps she had lost sight of the competing pressures to which they were exposed. While all of the coordinators recognized the importance of SMAD and affirmed their commitment to it, nevertheless, for them it was not the be-all and end-all. Nor could it be. There was too the perception that on occasion the project manager had failed to appreciate just how trying and demoralizing were the circumstances under which some of the coordinators were having to operate. In sum, the charge was that the project manager's single-mindedness was simultaneously a strength and a shortcoming. The following comment captures the feelings displayed by these highly committed educators.

> Sometimes the demands . . . made on us are quite unrealistic . . . We also are teachers and we also have a responsibility to the kids who we should be teaching our subject to . . . I'm a teacher, then I'm a head of department, and then I'm the SMAD coordinator.

More often than not these demands were of a bureaucratic nature and linked to accountability. Even some of the headteachers perceived that the, at times excessive, demands had jeopardized other aspects of coordinators' workloads. 'The biggest drawback has been the bureaucracy involved, to the detriment of the (coordinator's work in the) classroom', declared one of the heads. This was affirmed by one of the coordinators.

> I feel I've spent too much time on administering the budget and a lot of time on chasing things up . . . I have spent a lot of time on accounts rather than on curriculum development.

And as localized initiatives took off in the schools, other members of staff found themselves subjected to similar pressures. A head of department in one school noted:

> I have found some of the central administration to be both bureaucratic and not always efficient. There has not been enough awareness that someone in my position, in addition to organizing a revision centre, is also managing a number of teachers and teaching nearly a full timetable — therefore to be given 'urgent' demands for information on a regular basis has been unsettling and not always necessary.

Keith Pocklington

The SMAD School Coordinators

The project manager always intended that this group of nine teachers — one school appointed joint coordinators — should serve as a mutual support group; hence, the time and effort she invested in team-building. In the event, what materialized exceeded expectations, and can be said to have been a notable achievement of the project.

From a comparatively early stage a rapport was established which, over time, was built on and developed. There has been much exchanging of information and pooling of ideas, together with offering reassurance and support of a general nature. Issues have been thrashed out and awareness of practice in other schools has been raised. In addition, there have been times when group members have actively assisted one or more of their peers on a specific task e.g., refining some aspect of the Project Plan or identifying success indicators. Thus, in spite of some striking contrasts in personality, together with variation in the level and range of experience, all nine coordinators contributed substantially to the group, thereby enhancing its collective strength and influence. Furthermore, to the extent that individual coordinators encountered difficult and challenging circumstances, and even suffered reverses on occasion, having the support of this close group of peers proved to be vital.

The main tasks for which each coordinator assumed responsibility were envisaged as being to coordinate the production, implementation, monitoring and evaluation of their school's Project Plan, in conjunction with members of the SMAD working party. The Project Plan comprised the various initiatives identified as the means for attempting to raise pupil achievement, morale and motivation in the school.

What impact were the nine coordinators able to have in their respective schools, and what factors had a bearing on their effectiveness?

Appointing a named person in each school whose responsibility it was to stimulate and oversee particular developments certainly has proved significant to the degree of success achieved to date. Pressured as these people were — and in no way did the modest amount of release match the time demands of the role — it has meant that more attention and energy could be concentrated on SMAD than would have been the case had this simply been yet another responsibility tacked on to a senior teacher or deputy head's existing workload.

What did the coordinators contribute?

Various role components may be identified, not all of which were to be found in every case, nor to the same degree. They include:

- Establishing a SMAD working party. Thereafter, convening periodic meetings, providing leadership (including sustaining morale, and exercising responsibility for the work of its members).
- Formulating the Project Plan, in association with their line-manager and possibly other members of senior management, together with working party colleagues.
- Devising strategies for implementing the different elements of the Project Plan.
- Determining procedures for monitoring and evaluating progress. Maintaining oversight of progress overall.
- Gaining colleagues' support for and commitment to the initiative.
- Liaising with and supporting colleagues.
- Informing colleagues of developments, providing feedback on and publicizing events and initiatives.
- Organizing and possibly helping to deliver relevant inservice training.
- Managing day-to-day administration of the project, including expenditure.

What of the progress made?

As was noted earlier, different rates of progress have been realized across the eight schools. Why this should be so is a complex matter, reflecting: the circumstances obtaining in the schools, which are unique for each school, of course; the nature of what was being attempted in each of the schools, which has varied in scope and complexity; the extent of the support for the individual coordinator from senior managers; and the coordinator's effectiveness. (More will be said about this complex interplay of factors below.)

What factors were seen to have a bearing on the extent to which the efforts of the coordinators were instrumental in the degree of success achieved?

Firstly, the personal qualities that the postholders displayed. These include: being personable, reasonably outgoing and having good interpersonal skills; being able to motivate others and gain their commitment; and being enthusiastic, resilient and persevering.

Secondly, a coordinator's professional capabilities, which were seen to reflect their previous experience to a considerable degree. These embrace such considerations as experience in a managerial-cum-leadership capacity (e.g., as a head of department), the ability to think strategically, and possessing sound organizational skills. Of critical importance in this regard is the breadth of their experience, which showed considerable variation.

Thirdly, the value of relevant prior experience was strongly underlined: in particular, possessing a vision of what might be, and adopting a medium-term perspective; also, having the capacity to think and act strategically and tactically.

Fourthly, the status and credibility that the coordinator was able to command, and, as a consequence, the degree of influence they were able to wield. It was apparent that those who enjoyed head of department or senior teacher status, generally speaking, were in a stronger position to influence colleagues and to make things happen than were those of their peers who were on the equivalent of an 'A' or 'B' grade.

Fifthly, the condition of the school undeniably had a major impact on what the coordinator was and was not able to help bring about. Those schools that might be described as 'unhealthy' organizations — for example, characterized by weak management and leadership and a high turnover of staff, whose staff felt besieged, where simply surviving each week was sufficient of a goal in itself, and which contained substantial numbers of disaffected pupils — as a rule were the schools wherein the SMAD coordinators experienced the greatest problems.

What difficulties did the coordinators experience as they went about their task?

Firstly, irrespective of any prior relevant experience and the extent to which they were supported by more senior colleagues, the coordinators widely testified to the challenging nature of the role. Indeed, one aspect of which they were critical was the scope of the role and the manner in which it seemed to them that it had been allowed to grow virtually unchecked.

Secondly, most of the coordinators experienced difficulty in formulating the Project Plan. This was perhaps hardly surprising, in that for most it was an activity with which they were unfamiliar. The extent to which they struggled was tempered in those situations where they were well supported, but unfortunately not all were.

Thirdly, managing a fairly substantial budget also was outside the range of experience of most. Again, one or two were fortunate — for example, where the head or a school bursar provided assistance and assumed ultimate responsibility. Others, however, either were left to struggle or were left feeling disempowered, where a head assumed control or was reluctant to relinquish control in the first place.

Fourthly, the coordinators did not find it easy to build in effective, realistic and workable means of monitoring and evaluating the developments which occurred in their schools.

A fifth aspect, upon which the coordinators were more divided, concerns the capacity to develop and coordinate a project such as SMAD. This entails, among other things: having some ideas about promising lines of development; formulating strategies whereby ideas may be translated into action; ensuring that the specifics are not neglected yet simultaneously retaining sight of the whole; mapping out the intended course of events and keeping abreast of them; and having the means of determining whether they have been a success or not. A minority, typically the more experienced among the group, went on to acquit themselves superbly in this regard, through a combination of their inner resources and support, as necessary, from one or more senior colleagues. The others found it more difficult, and where the support of senior staff was limited or even lacking, then at times they experienced profound difficulty.

Despite being hard going at times, and although it exacted a heavy toll in terms of their own development, the experience proved invaluable, professionally as well as personally. One of the main ways in which the coordinators perceived they had gained was in developing a much broader awareness. Discharging the role of coordinator took them beyond considerations having solely to do with their school and department, and with teaching their subject to their pupils. In addition, it proved both energizing and empowering, and for some even helped to revive jaded careers. Interests were aroused, knowledge extended, a range of skills acquired or refined, and self-confidence was boosted.

Headteacher–Coordinator Partnership

It was the intention that the headteacher should act as the first line of support within school for the SMAD coordinator, with further support, as necessary, provided by other members of the senior management. In the event, one head opted to delegate this responsibility to one of his deputies, whilst in a number of other cases the intention was not realized, for various reasons. Accordingly, whilst the coordinators' need of support varied, only four out of the nine coordinators received the level and nature of support from the head or other senior managers that they felt they required. A few clearly were independent minded. They tended to be the more capable and proficient in the role. For these individuals it was entirely appropriate that support should be delivered mainly at arm's length. Of the remainder, some at least were among those most in need.

Where the intended partnership failed to materialize, this could reflect a number of things. Possibly the level of interest in and commitment to the scheme was on the low side. More commonly, however, it was indicative of the pressures to which the heads in question were already exposed, such that SMAD was not among their highest priorities. (A measure of the intensity of this pressure is that of the eight heads in post at the beginning of the project, two had been replaced some 12 months later. Further, one of the schools experienced no fewer than four different headteachers over the duration of the project. And at a third school the head took early retirement.)

In those schools where the coordinator was a member of the senior management team, this presented a naturally occurring forum in which concerns could be raised, guidance requested, and so forth. Two of the coordinators in fact were co-opted onto their school's senior management team, a move which was acclaimed by all parties. One of the headteachers whose decision it had been to take this action had no doubts as to its significance in ensuring that SMAD became an integral part of institutional development.

> I can't overestimate the importance I give to the total overview
> of the school that the senior management has, and SMAD being
> a part of this . . . Everything that goes on has got to be part of
> . . . the grand design for the school.

The SMAD Working Party

School coordinators were strongly encouraged by the project manager to convene a working party, whose task initially was to assist in the production of the Project Plan. Thereafter, their main function was to facilitate and oversee SMAD-related developments in the school. Coordinators were advised that these working parties should include representation from a range of subject areas and experience and, where possible, should also incorporate pupil representatives.

Some coordinators seemingly took to this idea with alacrity, seeing the working party as a potentially invaluable source of support. Others, however, appeared more reluctant. In that working party membership was voluntary, the readiness with which the party came together may be seen as indicative of the coordinator's standing in the school and the extent of his or her informal networks. It may also be a reflection of the level of energy within a school's teaching staff and of morale generally.

Working parties eventually were set up in all eight schools. The quality of their functioning showed a great deal of variation however. Where they worked really well, typically, it said a lot about the personalities and dynanism of the people involved. Their main contribution, quite apart from sharing the coordinator's workload, was in generating a multiplicity of ideas and suggestions for enhancing pupils' levels of achievement and motivation, together with sewing the seeds of change amongst immediate colleagues.

In some of the schools, a development of this nature represented a marked departure from past practice — there was no history of involving teachers in issues broader than simply teaching their subject. In turn, this was seen on occasion to delay the group's capacity to exert influence, in that it took time for those concerned to become accustomed to this way of working. The broader state that a school was in also could have a bearing on the functioning and the effectiveness of the working party. For instance, in one school, whose senior management was under immense pressure in the lead up to an Ofsted inspection, and where the issue of enforced redundancy amongst the staff proved both divisive and morale sapping, the working party disintegrated after a little over two terms, leaving the coordinator largely bereft of both in-house allies or support.

Other More General Factors that Aided Development

- That it was a borough-led initiative and implemented borough-wide, which brought with it a sense of, 'We're all in this together'. Furthermore, that SMAD was in line with developments at national level.
- That it was accompanied by considerable financial resources, a proportion of which had to be spent quite quickly. In so far as this went on material improvements to the school environment, it was popular with many students and staff, who saw immediate and tangible results.

- That its focus — namely, the emphasis on enhancing student learning, and the improvement of student attainment, achievement and morale — was seen to be pertinent by teachers and was popular with them.
- That it was a project that enabled school managers and teachers to introduce and implement developments of their choice and for which they could see the potential value — subject to the broad parameters of the project being observed. Furthermore, it was an initiative that recognized the professional knowledge and expertise of teachers.
- Co-opting the school coordinator onto the senior management team.
- A firm steer by the headteacher.
- The circumstances of the individual school; most especially, the overall stability of the organization and the quality of its management.
- The existence of tight central structures and organization, thereby harnessing the project to a school's central mission. In particular, an effective system of monitoring and geared to developmental — rather than bureaucratic — ends.
- The 'plan, do and review' approach embodied in the project, as a whole, systematically and rigorously applied.
- The combination of internally led change (via the school coordinator and the SMAD working party) and external stimulation, support and pressure (via the project manager).
- The importance attached to relevant inservice training; together with opportunities to visit schools outside the borough to observe and learn about interesting practice.

Factors Hindering Development

- The consequences of being exposed to the new form of inspection conducted by Ofsted. No fewer than four of the schools underwent an Ofsted inspection during the formal lifespan of the project — a reflection of the priority attached by Ofsted in its first year of operations to subjecting to close scrutiny schools that were known to be experiencing difficulties. One consequence of an impending inspection was felt to be the tendency for this to become the predominant consideration weeks and even months in advance, to the detriment of other matters.

- In some schools formulating the Project Plan took far longer than anticipated, — sometimes with a further delay in gaining authorization for what was proposed — resulting in a loss of motivation amongst often over-stretched professionals.
- The emphasis on process elements, e.g., developing sound relationships and teamwork, consulting extensively and building a sense of ownership, although of value, simultaneously served to defer the introduction of more tangible developments.
- The pressure to show immediate results.
- The limited progress to date in some of the schools in making SMAD truly an integral part of organizational development.
- The problems experienced in certain schools in being able fully to capitalize on the newly developed flexible learning bases.
- The limited progress made in augmenting teachers' expertise (through inset) in certain of the schools, particularly in respect of more flexible approaches to teaching and learning.
- The absence of relevant inset specifically for middle managers until comparatively late in the day — in part, a reflection of a lack of response to offers made by the project manager.
- The limited progress in sharing expertise within the schools; and in the process, perhaps helping to break down departmental barriers and identities.
- The apparent failure to plan, organize and implement thoroughly several of the initiatives mounted within certain schools. Alternatively, being overambitious at the outset.
- The degree of bureaucracy that a good many heads and teachers felt that SMAD brought in its wake. That said, however, in situations such as this where substantial sums of money are involved, there are no easy or obvious solutions to the problem of public accountability.
- The difficulties experienced in involving parents in a more substantial role in their offspring's education.

Developments in the Schools

Over and above what impact, individually and collectively, the coordinators, headteachers, working party colleagues and the project manager were able to have, in so far as successes were realized, this also was a consequence of the efforts of individual teachers for/in whom SMAD struck a chord, and who recognized here an opportunity which they could exploit. Some illustrations of how they were able to shape practice will become apparent as we focus now upon some of the lines of development that took place.

Developments Directly Affecting the Learning Environment of the School

On the whole, students and teachers alike appeared favourably disposed to the various improvements to the learning environment, including new facilities such as flexible learning bases, study areas and common rooms. There was abundant anecdotal evidence from students and staff that a more attractive and better equipped physical environment had served to promote more mature and responsible behaviour. 'If it's decent, people keep it decent', a teacher declared. And a pupil from the same school observed, 'It makes school a more welcoming place'. The general improvements to the physical environment were widely praised, popular and well-treated. The only reports of minor acts of vandalism came from a school that was facing some especially pronounced and intractable difficulties. As for specific developments, students were highly enamoured of the various flexible learning bases, the state of the decor and the equipment and facilities to be found in a number of these prompting a mixture of wonder, excitement and keenness to avail of what they had to offer. Here was a resource to which pupils were strongly attracted.

Undoubtedly, part of the reason for the generally positive reception had to do with the degree of consultation that took place, especially amongst the students. Indeed, in several schools the pupils themselves played a major part in organizing and conducting the process of consultation and, in a few instances, formulating a plan of action (including costing various options) to which this gave rise. Also relevant was the degree of trust vested in the students, including giving them responsibility for 'policing' the use made of the facilities.

Developments Directly Affecting Students

Revision centres and coursework clinics

The revision centres ran during the Easter holiday periods, and were mainly, though not exclusively, targeted at Year 11 students. Initially, they went ahead in seven of the schools, but such was their popularity with students, staff and parents alike, allied to their perceived effectiveness, that the eighth school soon followed suit.

It was common for someone other than the SMAD coordinator to exercise responsibility for their organization, and the quality of that organization would seem to have varied. They also differed in both scale and scope from school to school, although most organizers sought to ensure that at the very least the core curriculum subjects were represented. Coursework clinics in many respects were a spin-off, and reflected the success of the revision centres. They were similar in design and intent, though on the whole less extensive. They usually took place during half-term breaks, and had a similar target clientele (typically, Years 10 and 11).

The revision centres in particular represent one of the undoubted successes of the overall project. What was behind their popularity? The main advantages most commonly cited by students were as follows:

- They offered a forum within which schoolwork could be undertaken, including a certain amount of catching up. This was in contrast to the lack of facilities for studying in the home in many cases.
- The individual attention from teachers that was available and which could be tailored to specific needs.
- The calm and purposeful atmosphere that prevailed.
- Access to computers and other resources.
- The help received with study skills and exam techniques.

Teachers too were equally enthusiastic. It was widely held that the emphasis on working and studying diligently, together with the level of individual attention that could be provided, were crucial to the degree of success realized. In turn, this was seen to alter the whole ambience of these sessions, including pupil–teacher and pupil–pupil relations. (Many of the teachers who put on sessions referred to how enjoyable and stimulating an experience it had been for them also.) In addition, the generally smaller numbers meant that there was greater scope for teachers to foster relationships amongst the pupils. Indeed, a number of teachers in different schools were heard to state that the experience had led them to change their perceptions of certain students as a consequence of their good attendance and behaviour in this different-from-usual setting. All in all, teachers had few doubts that the revision centres had helped to enhance pupils' motivation and commitment toward attaining examination success.

There does appear to have been a tangible pay-off, in that a good many students subsequently attained better than expected GCSE examination grades. Table 6.1 puts the borough's examination results in context by comparing them with the results of other inner London boroughs between 1989 and 1994. Data provided by the borough's Research and Statistics section reveals that almost 52 per cent of the Year 11 pupils entered for GCSE examinations attended the Easter 1994 revision centre held in their school for at least some of the time. More importantly, these pupils had an average GCSE performance score a full 10 points higher than that of their peers who did not attend a revision centre at any stage (see Table 6.2). This is the equivalent of two GCSE 'C' grades per pupil. The differences in certain of the schools were even more striking. For instance, in one school the average GCSE points score of pupils attending compared to the score for those who did not attend was a full 16 points — equivalent to one grade 'B' and two grade 'C's per pupil! There is, in addition, other evidence available to suggest that those students who attended revision classes performed better at GCSE, regardless of their ability at entry to secondary school (see Table 6.3).

However, it should not be inferred from these findings that examination success is directly dependent on attendance at revision classes. That students in two of the schools performed exceptionally well, irrespective of whether they had attended the revision centre or not, rather gives the lie to such a simplistic interpretation, although it has to be said that both schools had a history of realizing high academic performance. The conclusion that may be drawn, however, is that some students in some of the schools do appear to have benefited from having experienced this additional provision. It does appear to be the case that making available such provision can have a critical effect on the level of attainment — as measured by public examinations — of certain pupils, typically those of average or below average ability and/or motivation. The positive impact of this provision characteristically was greater in those schools with a history of low academic achievement.

What cannot be determined with any certainty at this time is whether part of the reason for these measured differences in performance may stem from the tendency of the revision centres to attract a disproportionate number of the more highly motivated and able pupils anyway. However, in virtually every school, teachers who had been directly involved in some capacity or other were heard to remark on the range of students present. A key consideration here is that attendance was voluntary — although some teachers in some of the schools did target certain students. It should be said, however, that it was by no means the case that all who attended did so for positive reasons. Some were

Table 6.1: All borough schools compared with inner London: performance scores for 15+
GCSE pupils

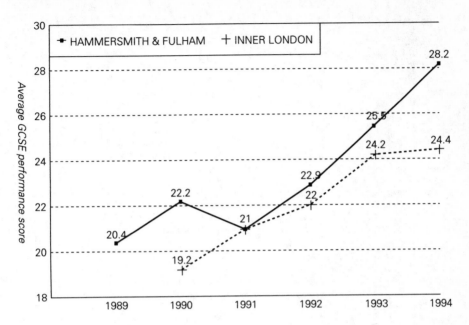

Table 6.2: Average GCSE performance score for all secondary schools by whether or not
pupils attended revision classes in 1994

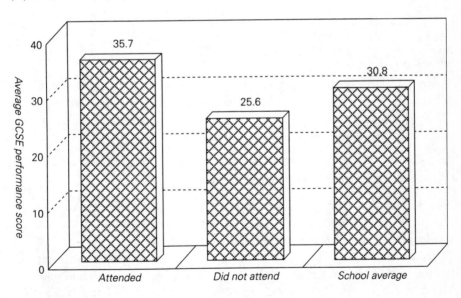

This analysis includes data on 758 pupils (391 attended 367 did not)
Pupils who were not entered for any exams are excluded
Produced by Education Dept R & S

Table 6.3: *All schools pupils' GCSE scores plotted against LRT scores by whether or not they attended revision classes*

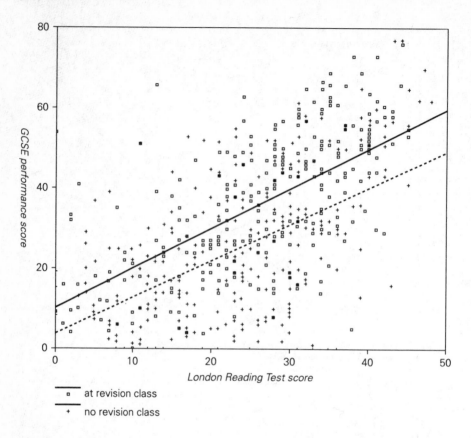

known to be there because they had nowhere better to go and nothing else to do. Also, we should not overlook the fact that there were plenty of students who failed to attend — over 48 per cent of Year 11 pupils who were entered for GCSE examinations.

Extension and enrichment classes

Additional voluntary extension and enrichment classes were mounted in seven of the schools, over the lunchtime period or after school. (In the eighth school they were introduced in the Autumn Term 1994.) The idea here was to extend or to supplement the normal school curriculum. Instances of the extension classes were either subject-based or were more general e.g., Homework Club. Examples of the latter (i.e.,

All tables produced by Research and Statistics Section, Education Department, Hammersmith and Fulham.

enrichment classes) were many and varied, broadly being interest based. In some of the schools such provision was introduced quite early in the lifespan of SMAD, and was expanded considerably over the next nine months or so. Schools also differed as to whether they offered mainly academic or mainly interest-based classes, or a mixture of the two. Typically, classes were open to all age ranges.

The reasons for pupils attending, and what they feel they are deriving from it, will vary to an extent, depending on the nature of the provision and the dominant ethos amongst pupil sub-groups, which itself would appear to vary across the schools. In the case of the subject-related classes, in those schools where there was moderate or good attendance, typically this was because pupils were experiencing difficulties with the subject and were looking for help, or simply wanted to catch up with coursework. Others were seeking to improve their work in preparation for forthcoming exams. Further reasons given, included the access to resources (including computers), and simple enjoyment of the subject.

However, not all of the schools would appear to contain what one teacher referred to as 'a culture of learning'. In one such school there was a marked difference in popularity between the subject-related extension classes and those which were interest-based. A teacher explained that the former tended to be looked down on as boring, and to be dismissed as 'just an extension of a lesson'. Also, pupils were perceived to be sensitive to losing face by being seen attending such classes.

For those classes which were interest-based however, the main reasons pupils gave for attending were a combination of curiosity — 'I wanted to try something new and different', one student wrote — and enjoyment of the activity in question. A reason commonly given for the general popularity of the extension and enrichment classes was that they attracted pupils from different age ranges and allowed for social interaction. As to how they felt they had benefited, students who had attended classes which were subject-related typically referred to having made progress with their studies, given the help of the teacher and perhaps having been able to use specialized learning resources and facilities. They also appreciated being able to work at their own pace rather than that of the class as a whole. For some, an important factor was the very different atmosphere that prevailed.

The view of teachers was similarly positive, and tended to emphasize the social dimension. 'I think it's very important that staff see pupils in a different light', declared one headteacher. A member of staff echoed the head's remark, 'Kids see you doing things that perhaps they didn't ever associate you with.' It was felt to introduce a different di mension to the student–teacher relationship, and thereby to strengthen it.

There was, however, one main cause for dismay associated with this element of the project. Some of the teachers who had become involved detected increasing reluctance, on the part of some senior colleagues and the project manager, to continue to sanction the more interest-based of the classes over time. One teacher explained what it was about the prevailing character of the extended day programme (largely interest-based) in her school that made it so pertinent to the pupils, and hence so popular with them. The intention had been to broaden students' experience and encourage social interaction, with a view to building a stronger sense of community within school.

> It's about making [pupils] feel a part of the school community ... They have problems socializing ... [Our pupils] don't want to spend their time after school doing what they see as 'school work' — they just want to have fun ... perhaps mix with different people, relate to the teacher on a different level ... For our kids, it's nice for them to do things they've not been able to do before.

This teacher maintained that although academic performance mattered, it ought not to be the sole consideration. To support this assertion the teacher referred to improvements that she detected in the school, and which she felt could be attributed, at least in some part, to the extended day programme.

> I think definitely the atmosphere has changed in a positive way. There are lots of students who can be quite difficult but whose behaviour has improved. It has something to do with the improved relationship between pupils and adults.

Occasions for celebration

Whilst efforts were made in all of the schools to take a more constructive line and accentuate the positive, at least two schools took this further and held public celebratory events e.g., of Black Achievement, of Women's Achievement. Although immensely time-consuming to organize, they proved a great success, raising pupil and teacher morale and helping to build a sense of community. As the head of one of the schools remarked:

The Black Achievers evening and the recent School Achievement afternoon contributed to the development of a positive school ethos, and put the spotlight on successful rather than disruptive students.

Curriculum Initiatives

In a number of the schools specific initiatives of various kinds were adopted in an effort to promote student attainment. Prominent among them were schemes aimed at enhancing literacy. By way of example, one school mounted a Readers and Writers Week on two occasions, a major aim of which was to promote reading within the school and across the curriculum. All students were given the opportunity to meet and work alongside a range of story writers, poets and performance artists. The emphasis was upon active forms of learning. It proved enormously popular with the pupils, many of whom produced work of an impressive standard. Of even greater significance for those teachers who organized the event was the transformation in pupil behaviour. It was thought that having additional adults other than teachers in the school had been the crucial difference. 'The kids rose to that', said one teacher. 'There was a buzz in the school for weeks afterwards', a second noted, adding that it had raised pupil morale and motivation. One of the organizers drew attention to the emphasis placed on focused learning for the week; it was insufficient simply for the pupils to be entertained by their artist visitors.

> You've got to give students a purpose to their learning. They discovered that they could, for example, write poems. Through discussing books and poems they were able to realize the importance and the value of what talk is and being able to use speech . . . Speaking and listening skills really were enforced. For instance, I was very pleasantly surprised by the way students were couching questions . . . It gave students [the chance] to be . . . socially articulate in all the ways we would expect students to be.

Alongside this ran two further initiatives: a tutorial libraries scheme; and a literacy project. The former was directed at Years 7/8 and consisted of encouragement for pupils to devote a portion of their tutor group time to reading. Resource materials were bought in for each tutor group to utilize. The literacy scheme was specifically targeted on some fifteen of the poorest readers (having a reading age of below seven) in Year 7. For in the region of 25 minutes daily they worked in groups of three with a member of staff on activities designed to improve reading, writing and spelling. The staff involved were provided with specialized training by an educational psychologist experienced in diagnosing pupils' specific difficulties with literacy and how to teach literacy skills in a structured way.

Significantly, of the two initiatives, it was the latter that was acclaimed as the more successful. Some quite remarkable gains were claimed by the head of Learning Support, who was one of the organizers e.g., that all pupils had improved their reading age by at least six months over the two terms for which the scheme ran, with an average improvement of 16 months. Asked about what lay behind the differing degrees of success of these two initiatives, this teacher identified the crucial importance of having someone to monitor practice closely. She had not been able to devote as much time to the tutorial libraries scheme as was seen to be necessary.

Another of the curricular initiatives mounted under the auspices of SMAD concerns those developments which come under the umbrella term, 'active approaches to learning'. Generally speaking, it has to be said that it is still early days — there were relatively few examples of such practice. However, individual teachers in a number of the schools were reported by the coordinators to be keen to get underway such practice and were planning small-scale pilot trials. An instance is provided by a head of history who, following on a SMAD-sponsored inset day on flexible learning at his school, developed a three week module on the Home Front in World War II. This teacher was careful not to make grandiose claims about what had been achieved, although he felt quite positive. He reported that pupils had been highly appreciative, and that in his view the module had stimulated enjoyment and motiva-. tion, and had led to some high quality work. An active learning centre had recently been established in the school which, in the long term, ought 'to facilitate an important enhancement of teaching and learning strategy, particularly in developing skills as independent learners and pupil motivation/commitment'.

Forms of Student Monitoring and Support

Various initiatives designed to provide personalized support for pupils were launched in a number of the schools, although strictly speaking, not all of them were funded under SMAD. Two schools in particular introduced schemes for delivering intensive support to students who were perceived to be at risk of failing to achieve to their potential.

In one of these schools, under the auspices of the project, pupil monitoring was targeted on Year 8 pupils who either were underachieving or were felt to be in danger of doing so. Each was assigned a 'mentor', a member of the school's senior management, with whom they met regularly e.g., fortnightly, usually on a one-to-one basis, for up to two terms. Various aspects of their schooling would be discussed on these occasions e.g., difficulties being experienced over particular subjects or teachers, the setting and marking of homework, the setting of targets, and keeping their school journal up to date.

The headteacher was enthusiastic about this practice: 'It gave them the target setting, focused their minds. They saw the importance of things . . . they saw the importance of all subjects.' She noted that it had both a symbolic value and the possibility of a practical pay-off. 'They felt important, felt they were being valued because they had an opportunity to discuss their work and the school in general.' However, a rather more mixed picture began to emerge as a result of having discussed this practice with a (admittedly small) sample of pupils. Though some reported that it had been of benefit — for instance, helping them to resolve minor difficulties associated with particular subjects and/or teachers, bringing about greater clarity in their thinking, raising self-esteem, generally 'keeping them on their toes' — others suggested that its value had been very limited. A particular concern expressed by several of the pupils was that of how far they felt able to confide in senior staff, especially in relation to talking honestly about teachers with whom they did not get on.

At the second school a similar scheme was mounted, this involving seven volunteer teachers, each of whom agreed to 'adopt' a Year 11 student who was adjudged to be a 'borderline' case. Here, the idea was that, with a little extra personal attention and support, students might be enabled to perform at a significantly better level in their GCSE examinations. Some eighteen students were helped in this way. The resulting practice would appear, however, to have been very variable. Some teachers adopted more than one pupil, perhaps not fully appreciating the time commitment entailed. Then again, although some staff did meet fairly regularly, and introduced a degree of structure into these sessions, others approached the task in a more *ad hoc* fashion. Meetings were infrequent, were called with little or no advance notice, and were largely unstructured. It also appeared to be the case that what those involved saw themselves providing and sought to achieve from these sessions differed quite markedly. Hardly surprising then that the degree of success realized varied from teacher to teacher.

Whilst the majority of the students would appear to have benefited to an extent, none the less it would seem that much of the scheme's potential remained unrealized. With hindsight, the coordinator recognized that perhaps it had been left too ill-defined and unstructured at the outset. Arguably, what was needed was time to discuss strategies and tactics, the issues likely to arise, and procedures for monitoring the practice. There might even have been a need for formal skills training. In addition, the overall practice was not subjected to systematic and close monitoring.

Student Consultation

A more general feature of the project had to do with strengthening procedures for student consultation. A number of the schools already had in place a means whereby the views of students could be heard, typically in the form of a student or school council. There were reports from some of these schools of the council's remit having been extended as a consequence of participation in SMAD, and in general their importance — and hence significance — would appear to have increased. Other schools that did not have a school council saw this as an opportune time to introduce one. It became commonplace for year group representatives to canvass the views and requests of their constituents and report back to the full council. Although much of this consultation was directed at suggestions for improving the physical environment of schools, nevertheless in certain of the schools the students engaged with some substantive issues — ways of reducing the incidence and the effects of bullying for example, or the development of codes of behaviour in the playground and corridors. Interestingly, however, nowhere did it appear to have extended to debating issues to do with teaching and learning itself, which, arguably, represents the acid test of student responsibility and participation.

Students certainly appreciated being asked for their ideas and opinions, especially as it became apparent that these were being carefully considered and often acted on. Also, it signified recognition that they were being accorded respect and trusted more. And for those students who took an active part, it proved an invaluable opportunity for personal development e.g., growth in confidence and self-esteem.

Changes to the Ethos of Schools

An extensive national survey of secondary schools, conducted by the University of Keele, has underlined the need to change the dominant culture of the pupil peer group from its present disposition of being opposed to studying and achieving, coupled with tolerating — if not actively engaging in — disruptive behaviour in the classroom, to one where motivation to work hard and expectations of success are the norm. What evidence is there of actions taken under SMAD having had a positive impact upon the school climate or ethos?

There was some confirmation from teachers, more especially those with direct involvement in the project, of improved behaviour among students. For example, a number of teachers admitted to having been pleasantly surprised by how responsibly the students had behaved when given an opportunity to exercise responsibility, e.g., when asked to suggest ways in which the school environment might be enhanced. Among the perceived improvements were:

- More mature and responsive behaviour
- Growth in students' self-esteem
- Better motivated pupils
- Stronger and healthier relations between staff and students and within the body of students.

In What Respects has Progress been more Limited?

Curriculum Differentiation and Active Approaches to Learning

In general, progress in implementing curriculum differentiation and active approaches to learning has been slow, and achievements to date therefore limited. Indeed, in three of the schools it would be difficult to find evidence of SMAD having had much, if any, effect upon teaching and learning up to now. Significantly, in each case, specific initiatives having to do with teaching and learning were not prominent in the Project Plans of these schools. However, that this is an under-developed aspect of practice is recognized in the most recent report of the chief inspector.

Differentiated teaching and learning is not fully satisfactory in any [secondary] school. Some aspects are more effective in individual departments but overall this is weak and needs close attention in 1994–95. (Annual Report 1993/94: *Part A – The Chief Inspector's Report*, Education Department)

Making further progress on this front is likely to be slow and to require effective leadership, for as the head of one of the schools observed: 'I think there's a great cultural change to be made over things like flexible learning'. Nevertheless, in at least half of the schools the foundations for flexible learning now appear to have been laid.

Work with Parents and Forms of Mentoring Involving Adults other than Teachers

Both of these areas were flagged early on by the project manager, but despite expressions of interest by several coordinators, in the event only in two schools was any headway made on the first of these areas.

At the first school, SMAD funding was used to set up a Home Link scheme, whereby parents of the then Year 7 pupils undertook to reinforce reading for pleasure in the home. After two terms, it was felt that the practice generally was working quite well. In the second of these schools, progress to date has been limited, although longer term it could lead to some very exciting developments. Here, as a consequence of the school's poor image and standing in the community, the first of three sessions held to date was of the order of a PR exercise. Thereafter, the focus of discussion increasingly has been channelled toward identifying ways in which a parent–teacher partnership could be established. One suggestion from parents was that they might become actively involved in the school's literacy scheme. It was also hoped that at some stage parents and employers might serve as role models for students.

The most common reason teachers gave for the failure to get some form of parent partnership scheme off the ground was lack of time. However, at one school the plans were scuppered by staffing problems. A further problem is that many of the schools have widely scattered and diverse (in terms of ethnic and socio-economic composition) catchments. Among the other difficulties the teachers face are:

- that it entails an inordinate amount of time to set up and organize such practices;
- that they are high risk, and hence require a good deal of confidence on the part of teachers;

- that there is little in the way of existing practice to serve as a guide, particularly at secondary school level.

As for the second area, entailing the deployment of adults from the wider community in a mentoring capacity, late on in the life of the project a small pilot scheme got underway, this involving one of the schools and staff recruited through the school's links with local industry. This innovative practice would appear to command immense potential, but it is far too early to gauge how it is working out in practice.

Some Key Issues and Questions That the Project has Raised

1. In those schools that are experiencing substantial problems, on the whole senior managers and teachers have found it difficult fully or readily to capitalize on the project — for all manner of reasons, not least of which would seem to be the sense of acute pressure they are under, the many competing demands on their time, and the often low morale among the staff. It would appear that the mind-set of teachers and managers who are struggling and under severe pressure is such that they get locked into day-to-day survival and are unable to raise their sights beyond the immediacies in order to think strategically. This begs the question of whether improvement initiatives such as SMAD are only suited to average or better than average schools — or at least schools that are not experiencing serious problems? And if so, what can be done, if anything, for those schools whose needs are most pronounced?

2. What pace to move at? A good deal of time was invested in establishing sound foundations, yet this took up considerable time, and there was relatively little tangible evidence to show for it. And all the while time was ticking away. It made for enhanced pressure, which all those most closely involved — the school coordinators and the project manager — felt very acutely.

3. As an external change agent — in this instance, the project manager — how to strike a balance between driving a project forward and allowing the 'insiders' to have a strong say in shaping it. Also, the emphasis placed on process elements (i.e., building the internal capacity to deliver change). Is this realistic in a scheme of such limited

duration? Furthermore, how far should an external change agent intervene in schools which appear to be taking a long time to make any headway? The dilemma is that to intervene risks no longer being true to guiding tenets and principles; and yet not to intervene may lead to failure.

4. What is the balance to be struck between considerations having to do with teaching and learning and the conditions of the workplace? Invariably, both are relevant in any attempt at school improvement.

5. How best to marry 'bottom up' developments to senior management initiated and led development? For instance, how to ensure that the pioneering flexible learning practices based on individual teachers, or possibly departments, become central to whole school growth?

6. Might the rate at which initiatives 'took' in schools have been increased had training and support been targeted on teams of staff in the schools, rather than, in the main, the coordinator and headteacher? Furthermore, if it can be established that this is a desirable objective, how might it be made feasible when, if the experience of SMAD is anything to go by, being able to guarantee time out of school for just the head and coordinator proved highly problematic?

7. What balance to strike between those initiatives that are tangible and more likely to have a relatively quick pay-off, e.g., revision centres, and those which are less tangible but more fundamental, e.g., inservice training and other measures designed to enhance teacher expertise?

8. How to demonstrate a difference, especially in a project of relatively short duration, i.e., what evidence to gather and how?

9. Under SMAD, various promising developments have taken place in certain schools, and yet their wider potential, even within those schools let alone across all eight schools, remains largely unexploited. How might these successful features be capitalized on for the wider good?

10. How best to ensure that progress to date is not wasted but is built on? How to continue to support such an initiative when the main pump-priming elements — the project manager and the financial resources — have gone?

11. In some quarters it is strongly felt that the crucial issue in raising student attainment and achievement has to do with raising the status of

schoolwork in the minds of some pupils and especially their parents/ guardians. Does this view have merit? And if so, what can be done?

Overall Conclusions

On the whole, the SMAD project can be said to have achieved its objective of establishing the foundations for raising student levels of attainment, achievement and morale — no mean feat for a comparatively short-lived initiative. Foundations have been laid in all of the schools, although they vary in extent and depth. In some schools — at least three — one can feel confident that developments which have been set in train will be taken forward and extended. In two, possibly three, other schools this may happen, given the necessary leadership and perhaps external support. In at least two schools, however, one has serious doubts. If it is to occur, stronger leadership from inside these schools will be required, together with continued and active support from the LEA and others.

At this stage it is well-nigh impossible to specify what the project has achieved in quantifiable terms. Indeed, being able to attribute any measurable improvement to the overall project, or to a particular project component, is likely always to prove elusive. This is not to rule out attempts to measure increased achievement or other forms of improvement, or to identify associations between certain outcomes and specific project elements. For the time being, however, this would be premature and thus unfair; SMAD deserves to be judged on its terms, and in accordance with its parameters. It was envisaged as a piece of pump-priming. Accordingly, it is only right to assess its achievements in terms of evidence of progress being underway. Also, this is being realistic.

What SMAD is about in many respects is little short of an attempt to change school culture. Enough is known from the burgeoning research literature on school improvement and the management of change to know that this takes time — typically, three to five years; yet the timescale of SMAD has been a mere 24 months, a substantial proportion of which essentially was preparatory.

The continued unfolding of the various strands of development should be monitored over the next three years or so, at the end of which it would be more appropriate to seek to answer some hard-edged questions; notably, whether or not student attainment (in terms of examination grades) has continued to show improvement across the board. A good proportion of the initiatives in the schools have been focused on lower school pupils — an investment in the future, if you will. By that time these pupils will have worked their way through the school, and any benefits that may be attributed to SMAD ought to show up more clearly. Baseline measures of pupil functioning, which are being gathered by the schools and the LEA, ought to prove informative here. In addition, thought needs to be given as to how other relevant aspects of 'improvement', e.g., pupil behaviour, attendance, self-esteem, independence and self-reliance, might be assessed.

Looking to the immediate future, more than one respondent voiced this fear: 'The great danger is that the SMAD impetus will disappear.' How then to ensure that it does live on? The LEA is committed to continuing to provide support, *albeit* on a different basis and scale, and in a different form. For their part, the headteachers of all eight schools have indicated their desire to continue working in partnership with the local authority and with each other, and to build on what has been started. A dialogue is underway to determine how intent can best be translated into action. That there will continue to be a need for direct support from the local authority seems inescapable. How much support, and what form this might take, is harder to say. Encouragement and guidance will continue to be needed, e.g., in relation to the spread of active approaches to learning.

For much of the project's life-span members of the inspectorate deliberately did not play a great role in promoting or supporting it — in part, a reflection of the project having its own manager. However, their involvement grew in the later stages — a development that needs to continue. It is understood that linkage with the inspectorate has now been formalized, and that all secondary inspectors will assume some responsibility as part of their link role, with the acting chief inspector having oversight and coordinating the overall practice. In addition, possibly the borough inset programme might be revised so that it reflects some of the practices and issues relevant to SMAD, e.g., debate about 'value added' — what is meant by the term, how do you actually build it in, and how do you measure its effect? Furthermore, if earmarked funding from schools' delegated budgets could be channelled to enable further attention to be devoted to developing curriculum modules and learning resources based on the principles of active learning, this would appear to be a particularly sound investment.

And what of the schools? Several things matter here. First and foremost, the need to ensure that the key elements from SMAD are integral to a school's development plan. Also, the active support and stimulation from the head is critical. Arguably, in addition, school governors have a part to play. To date, governors appear to have had little, if any, involvement, this despite repeated overtures from the project manager. Making SMAD part of the School Development Plan immediately places it within the realm of the governing body, not least because governors will be responsible for authorizing investment in certain lines of development. In addition, however, there may well be aspects on which governors could take a lead or play an active part, e.g., being involved in the capacity of mentor, perhaps parent governors might become involved with reading and literacy schemes, and fund raising to allow specific initiatives to continue (most obviously, the revision centres). Whatever the particular initiative, the importance of delegating responsibility for that practice to a named individual or even a small team, in order to provide the necessary drive and support, and to monitor developments as they unfold, has been confirmed under SMAD. Increasingly, attention is likely to fall on individual departments, which are at the heart of teaching and learning. In this regard, it is important that management development training for middle managers commenced in the later stages of the project. This ought to have direct implications for enhancing the quality of teaching and learning within departments — for example, through the introduction of closer monitoring of teachers' and departmental practices, together with tighter monitoring of pupil performance.

One of the schools had introduced a well-structured system of departmental review, whose merits would appear deserving of wider adoption. Among other things, this ought to strengthen leadership within departments, foster teamwork, stimulate further developments in how staff approach teaching and learning and, overall, enhance the quality of the work undertaken.

The same school was exploring the notion of 'improvement teams' — groups of staff which come together for a set period of time and with a specific remit, and answerable to an overall coordinator of development or a projects group. It is worth underlining too that in several of the schools the flexible learning base either was not fully operational or had only recently commenced functioning. These represent a rich resource that holds a strong attraction for pupils. It is imperative that this is fully capitalized on; they must not be allowed to become just another part of the furniture, as it were, once the initial sheen wears off. Inset has a crucial part to play in this regard.

In conclusion, the local authority is to be commended for manifesting active leadership in seizing the initiative and mounting this project — and thereby focusing attention on teaching and learning. At a time when the scope of so many LEAs for stimulating and facilitating development of any kind has been seriously eroded, this adds to the achievement. In the words of one of the many respondents, 'In general, SMAD has provided: finance, framing, facilitation and "push".' Only a local authority could have attempted such an enterprise and on this scale. It was a radical and a brave step to take, and is fully deserving of praise. It has ensured that much needed developments in many of these eight schools are well on the way. The significance of the project is all the greater in that there is an important debate that is taking place nationally upon the issue of school improvement. It is crucial that schools and LEAs be active participants in this debate and, ideally, involved at the leading edge of this practice as it evolves. This is all the more true of inner-city boroughs such as Hammersmith and Fulham, where the nature and scale of the challenges facing schools and LEAs are so much greater.

Appendix

Methodology

The principal method of data gathering for the evaluation was the semi-structured interviewing of key participants. These were:

- The SMAD school coordinators
- The headteachers
- The project manager.

There were three main rounds of visits to schools: Summer 1993; late Autumn/early Spring of 1994; and Summer 1994. On each occasion the coordinator was interviewed about developments, and usually the headteacher was also involved. In addition, interviews were held with a range of staff who had become directly involved with the project as it unfolded, e.g., SMAD working party members, teachers to whom responsibility for specific elements of the project had been delegated. Also, students in six of the eight schools were interviewed (either in pairs or small groups) about their experience of SMAD and any benefits it had brought them. In the case of the project manager, there was a mixture of frequent informal conversations and periodic formal interviews. Finally, representing the LEA, both the then chief inspector and the director of education were interviewed.

Alongside the interviews with key participants, there were three other sources of information. Firstly, attendance at the two residential conferences, mainly in the role of non-participant observer. Secondly, a questionnaire to a random sample of teachers drawn from all eight schools, principally with a view to ascertaining whether SMAD had impacted on practice, and if so, how. Thirdly, examination of relevant documentation, including statistical information provided by the LEA Research and Statistics unit.

Epilogue *The* Schools Make a Difference *Project*

Patrick Leeson

When a project of this kind is used as a pump-primer to bring about change, the key question is, what will continue to be implemented in the longer term? The SMAD project was a high profile, well-resourced initiative that operated for a relatively short period of time. It brought with it high levels of motivation and activity from the participating schools and teachers, and included a range of experiences for staff and pupils. The project had ambitious goals: to lay the foundations for raising standards of achievement; and to make teachers and schools more effective. It was to be a learning exercise and not a prescriptive package, an opportunity for the schools to define their own needs and take their own focus for development. It did not set out to be a particularly curriculum- or classroom-focused change although clearly it was rooted in improving the quality of pupils' learning. These features had the advantage of providing a certain amount of clarity, a common direction and a fairly open agenda with the possibility of schools seeing some tangible, practical improvements to their environments in the early days.

In this way, I think, SMAD overcame a number of difficulties that frequently accompany the early days of development projects. There was not too much complexity or prescriptiveness, it was easily accepted, the needs it addressed were recognized by teachers, the capital resources provided practical results and all the schools could participate in a way meaningful for them. At the same time, the project, from its earliest days, promoted the underlying thinking and learning about school effectiveness that was to inform the change process in the schools. Attempting major developments in this way, to the life and environments of schools as a whole, can sometimes be over-reaching but it can also generate more significant and lasting teacher change.

The context into which the project was introduced also provided some of the ingredients for a successful start. Hammersmith and Fulham is a small LEA where contacts and communication between schools, if not already established, can be promoted easily; where the small number of secondary schools does not create problems of size and unmanageability; and where all the schools, whatever their differences, can share the agenda of raising achievement in an inner-city situation. The starting point was also a well-established partnership between the LEA and its schools, allowing a certain ease in the process of consultation and negotiation about the nature and the steering of the project.

It is well known that the features and context of a project's initiation have a strong influence on what it achieves and how lasting the changes will be. We not only sought improvements but we wanted them to be incorporated into the working practices of the schools. In seeking to comment on what these lasting changes are, and on what has been incorporated into the work of the LEA and the schools, it may not be surprising that the most notable outcomes in my view are to do with ethos and beliefs. The SMAD project was primarily about a message that the school could make a real difference — that a number of features of the school's organization, ethos and culture can influence the effectiveness of the school in raising pupil achievement. Without doubt the apparent open-endedness of the project's early start allowed the LEA and the schools to learn more about and define school effectiveness. It helped to create a common agenda and language to talk about school improvement, and there are now clearer expectations for guiding and measuring practice in the schools. In this sense the most lasting and deep-rooted outcome of SMAD that we can continue to build on is a shift in organizational culture. This is of great significance in an inner-city context where teacher expectations and beliefs about what is possible are the things that make a real difference to young people. SMAD became that classic kind of project, which is difficult to create, that helps to plan and motivate from without and works to guide and orchestrate what may be happening within the school. In creating such a strong culture of its own, it helped to develop the culture of the LEA and its capacity as an organization to promote innovation.

This is not to say that all the participating schools are noticeably different and that there has been a lasting shift in the belief systems of the majority of the teachers involved in the project. Indeed, there are some schools continuing to experience considerable problems. However it is fair to say that learning and improvement processes have been established in the schools, and there is a recognition that change and improvement are the main task. Although SMAD was an episode which came to an end it was not simply one event among many, it has strengthened processes in the schools and in the LEA. There is a stronger basis now for planning for change; better experience and skill in the use of planning techniques and processes; a number of teachers and pupils have action plans and targets; senior and middle managers see their role as one of coaching and training as well as supervising and managing; and there is more attention to the quality of outcomes. We have many of the ingredients for schools and the LEA to be better places of learning for young people and adults. In some cases these changes are not even very conscious but are becoming slowly more embedded in the ways in which the schools work.

The SMAD project promoted supportive structures for students that many teachers also recognize as needs for themselves. The project fostered student mentoring, action planning and target setting, more use of independent learning, additional support through revision centres and homework clinics, enhancements to student facilities, and extended day activities. In doing so, the project also highlighted the need for teachers to build success and to improve working processes for themselves. Schools used 'critical friend' arrangements for peer observation in the classroom, more structured and helpful line management, improved team work, team and individual action planning, and the school coordinator's role was to motivate staff and communicate ideas. In other words, there has been an emphasis on the quality of relationships between and among pupils and teachers, without which it is difficult to improve teaching and learning. Even in the schools that are continuing to experience difficulties, some of these processes have begun to make a difference to the quality of the work and to the outcomes achieved by some pupils and staff.

Set against this drive to create improving schools, there has been a background of other complex change in terms of implementing the National Curriculum and assessment, and of moving further down the road of full delegation under local management. In addition many teachers have perceived a shift in LEA support towards a greater emphasis on monitoring. To some minds, these developments have been out of step with the nature of the SMAD project. This is a partial view and belies the project's goal of helping schools to manage and understand all the changes expected of them, the insistence that pressure and support are needed in a balanced way for any development to succeed, and the project's use of monitoring to highlight successes and problems. While it was agreed that the LEA inspectorate would not be involved in the day-to-day management of the project, all link inspectors were involved in supporting its processes and monitoring progress. A major goal of the LEA is to promote self-evaluating schools, and the inspectorate operates much of the time on the basis of monitoring school development plans in partnership with each institution. The project created another clear focus for this approach to be used to extend the capacity of each school to monitor and evaluate its own progress. An outcome that is important for the continuation of SMAD's work is the realization on the part of participants that major external change like the National Curriculum has to be adapted and managed internally, and needs certain conditions to be taken on board at all, and that all improvement needs to use internal and external monitoring as a management tool.

Looking to the future, one of the most healthy signs as the project came to a close was the decision by the participating schools to continue many of the project's activities. The headteachers have appreciated the value of their own joint inservice training and continue to meet and work collaboratively, at times with the involvement of the director of education and other officers. The LEA has responded to the 1995–96 GEST (Grant for Education Support and Training) category on school effectiveness by providing a comprehensive programme of support to schools. This is based on the local authority's account of the features of effective schools and forms part of the ongoing work following the SMAD project. As part of this all the schools are committed to developing further their use of flexible learning and the LEA has made it a priority in the GEST funded work, particularly on Key Stage 4 and preparations for GNVQ (General National Vocational Qualifications). The schools will continue to provide extended day and revision and homework clinics, which are known to have had a noticeable impact on the achievements and attitudes of the students attending. The LEA Research and Statistics section will use the information about students attending Easter revision centres in all the secondary schools as part of the analysis of GCSE examination results this year. These results in turn are used to set further achievement targets with each school for the succeeding year.

In most situations, student mentoring and action planning are being extended to include other year groups as well as students in Years 10 and 11. It is noticeable that schools are prioritizing these processes in terms of teacher time, and many have revised the role of tutors and have developed their function to monitor and plan for individual pupils' progress. Schools report that pupils' responses are generally very positive and note an improvement in motivation and effort as a result. The LEA is supporting this work through training for tutors, through developments in careers education, and a working group that is focusing on curriculum progression 14–19.

For some time the effectiveness of middle managers has been a specific focus for schools, supported by the LEA and the SMAD project in particular. The management development programme for heads of department and heads of year is continuing, with a core LEA programme supplemented by additional sessions and activities provided in each school. This has been carefully arranged to ensure the development opportunities are incorporated into the line-management processes in the school and are closely related to specific aspects of the role of the participating teachers. Each of these teachers has been asked to create their own management development plan and to evaluate their own progress, based an agreed tasks to be carried out in the school. In this way the focus is on institutional development and once again there is the recognition that the change depends on influencing the daily activities of teachers in the work place.

In conclusion, the SMAD project in Hammersmith and Fulham grew out of, and has left behind, and LEA that is taking seriously the business of becoming more effective in achieving educational change. It is a professional business that has its own skills and knowledge which have to be acquired through experience and learning by LEAs and by schools. At the root of this effort is the complicated task of creating certain relationships and ways of working, a culture that is based on some shared assumptions about teaching and learning, and quite systematic ways of planning, implementing and monitoring that involve all the participants. SMAD highlighted, extended and demonstrated the efficacy of these processes, and in that sense more than any other the project has very active continuation.

List of Contributors

Donna Drake began her teaching career in 1984 in an 11–18 mixed comprehensive in Croydon. In 1987 she moved to the London borough of Southwark where she became second in charge of English at Kingsdale school. She joined St Mark's school as head of English in 1992 and became a member of the senior management team when she took up the role of the SMAD coordinator.

Joan Farrelly started teaching in 1955. Most of her teaching was in special educational in both the primary and secondary sector. She had experience of teacher training, community education and the ILEA inspectorate before being appointed deputy director/chief inspector in the new LEA of Hammersmith and Fulham in 1989. She retired from this post in 1994 but is still involved in a variety of education causes.

Sue Gregory started her teaching career in 1981 at Sir William Collins school in the ILEA. She has worked in three other inner-London schools teaching a range of humanities subjects. She is currently head of humanities at Burlington Danes School.

David Lees graduated in Natural Science from Queens' College Cambridge in 1976 and took a PGCE course at Bath University in 1977. Since then he has taught in secondary schools in Buckinghamshire, Bristol and Wimbledon before become deputy head at Burlington Danes School in 1990.

Patrick Leeson started teaching English and drama at St Edmond Campion School, Oxford in 1978. He became a head of department and subsequently worked with the Oxfordshire Advisory Service where he had responsibility for coordinating evaluation and research. In 1987 he became adviser for Language and Communication in Croydon and moved to Hammersmith and Fulham as a senior inspector in 1990. He is currently acting chief inspector.

Lesley Mortimer taught German and Latin in north Surrey schools for nine years while also holding posts of pastoral responsibility. She was deputy head of Drayton Manor High School in Ealing for eight years and has been head of St Mark's CE School since 1990.

Kate Myers is an Education Consultant. She was the Project Manager of the Schools Make A Difference (SMAD) project in the London borough of Hammersmith and Fulham. She has previously been a head of house and head of year in an ILEA comprehensive school; ILEA coordinator of the Schools' Council's Sex Differentiation project; an Advisory Teacher; Director of the SCDC/EOC Equal Opportunities project; and a Senior Inspector in the London borough of Ealing. She is a Registered Inspector and and an Associate Director of the International School Effectiveness and Improvement Centre, Institute of Education, University of London. She is currently coordinating the School Improvement Network at the Institute and undertaking the Doctor of Education Degree (EdD) at the University of Bristol.

Keith Pocklington worked at the National Foundation for Educational Research (NFER). In 1983 he became a Senior Research Associate at the University of Cambridge. Since 1986 he has been a freelance consultant conducting evaluations of a wide range of innovative programmes and practices, mainly, though not exclusively, within the field of Education. Most recently, he has been involved in two major national studies funded by the DFE, of Effective Management in Schools, and a pilot scheme of Mentoring for New Headteachers, in conjunction with colleagues from the National Development Centre of the University of Bristol. With Dick Weindling, his partner in CREATE Consultants, he is currently engaged in development work involving five schools drawn from two LEAs, with the aim of enhancing school effectiveness.

Christine Whatford began her career as a teacher of history at Elliott School, ILEA, where after also being head of history, head of house and senior teacher, she became deputy head. From 1983 to 1989 she was the head of Abbey Wood School in south London. She has been the director of education in the London borough of Hammersmith and Fulham since 1989.

Index

Index

Thomas, S. 7
Tomlinson, Sally 59
Tropp, L. 12
tutorial system 37, 105
TVEI 71, 83, 91
Two Towns project 13

United States of America 1, 19, 29

'value added' 7, 12, 28, 51, 154
van Velzen, W. 11
vandalism 138

visits 32, 52–3, 61, 78, 91, 95, 100,
    136

Wakefield 100
Williams, Paul 64
'Women's Achievement' 64, 113, 144
working parties 82, 87–8, 97,
    112–13, 126, 130–1, 134–6, 156

youth service 30–1

Zeneca 51, 101